SIMPLE MACHINES
MADE SIMPLE

SIMPLE MACHINES MADE SIMPLE

RALPH E. ST. ANDRE

1993
TEACHER IDEAS PRESS
A Division of
Libraries Unlimited, Inc.
Englewood, Colorado

I dedicate this book to all those out there who truly believe that
science is hot,
and who have helped to verify this hypothesis, especially
Susan and Mr. Bill.

TEACHER IDEAS PRESS
A Division of Libraries Unlimited, Inc.
P.O. Box 6633
Englewood, CO 80155-6633
1-800-237-6124
www.lu.com/tip

Library of Congress Cataloging-in-Publication Data

St. Andre, Ralph E.
  Simple machines made simple / Ralph E. St. Andre.
  xix, 150 p. 22x28 cm.
  ISBN 1-56308-104-0
  1. Simple machines. I. Title.
TJ147.S72 1993
621.8'11--dc20   93-23388
                                        CIP

CONTENTS

PREFACE

Simple machines help us do work by trading force for distance.

In my experience of teaching science and helping to develop science programs for more than two decades, a unit on simple machines would be voted least likely to succeed. I have watched this unit be used as trading stock by teachers of four different grade levels. "We'll trade you one simple machines for two biologies and a draft pick to be named at a later date...."

The reasons for the demise of simple machines units are all too common. "There just isn't time." "The activities are really dumb." "I can't find the materials." The truth of the matter is that simple machines are not simple for most people and that the explanation of why the things work is just beyond their grasp. Not knowing any better, and never feeling very badly about not knowing the whys, teaching simple machines never really created any personal hardship.

Do yourself a favor right now if any of this feels familiar and repeat after me: "Simple machines help us do work by trading force for distance." Now have your group do it chorally. (It seems to work best if you break the statement into two parts at first: "Simple machines help us do work" and "by trading force for distance.") Then chorally chant the complete statement. If you do this until it is rote for both yourself and your group, you have overcome the greatest hurdle in teaching the unit. Your personal and professional experience will lead you through the materials management and other related stresses of teaching science.

Believe it or not you already have all of the technical information that you need for teaching the unit. Whenever it comes time to discuss the results, all you have to say is "Simple machines...." (This phrase will soon come to haunt you and your class, but the point will be well made.) Then trace the path of the force and the path of the load to demonstrate that the force is always traveling farther than the load if there is positive mechanical advantage. See how simple that was?

By the way, the greatest part of my budget for science for years has been spent on masking tape and paper clips. These are materials that most administrators don't question too heavily in the budget. Rubber bands and rulers are usually pretty easy to come by, too. What else could you possibly need to teach science, right? It is hoped you will notice, when you go through the materials list for each of the activities, that there are very few pricey or esoteric items required for this vision of the well-appointed science laboratory.

Have you taught your group the phrase "Simple machines help us do work by trading force for distance" yet? If not, you had better get cracking—you're already a lesson behind!

□
INTRODUCTION

This book is intended to make science fun for both you and your students. It is the result of a serious number of years of teaching simple machines as a unit, a number of years I never thought possible to survive without being placed on life support. If my intentions are honorable, then you should be able to hold this book in one hand and teach with the other. If nothing else, you should develop a really strong arm!

A lot of information has been infused into this book, and it would be unfortunate if you missed any of it by the artful way I have incorporated so many cutting edge elements. So you won't miss anything, this introductory overview has been prepared.

If you are blocking off a time period that you are willing to commit to simple machines, you should plan on at least six to eight weeks. During that time you will need at least three 30- to 45-minute periods each week with a little extra time for serendipity because of the enthusiasm that is sure to be generated by your immersion in simple machines.

The book has been divided into nine chapters. Each of the content sections features a teacher introduction designed to provide a generative content base. That information will reappear in smaller pieces in each of the activities, and then again as part of the discussion of the results. After the background information is a series of interactive experiences for you and your students to sample. Each has been tried out with at least 20 different classes of about 30 students. Activity and assessment sheets are provided for your duplicating enjoyment and to take a little of the pain out of the job. The latter chapters of the book are devoted more to the teaching and learning environment. Included are such things as ideas for bulletin boards and learning centers that you might find useful.

Now let's take a brief look at each of the book's nine chapters. (By the way, if you did not read the preface and went right to this introduction, you have missed the first and most important lesson [just as a reminder: Simple machines help us do work by trading force for distance] that you can teach yourself and the students about simple machines. Do it now before you go on! The section closes with an overview of assessment tools that are embedded in the content sections. Most of this authentic assessment stuff for interactive science programs is only at a research stage nationally and internationally. It is worth your while to try some of it.)

The actual equipment for experimenting with simple machines is very pricey and, consequently, is one of the most common stumbling blocks for teaching simple machines. In chapter 1, you will find out how your students can make their own equipment at little or no cost with easily found materials.

Chapter 2 explores the world of levers. It is loaded with anticipatory sets, activities, extension activities, functional art, and much more.

You will be taken through a number of activities for the wheel and axle and all of its variations in chapter 3. I consider pulleys and gears to be a modification of the wheel and axle and not separate simple machines as they are treated in some resources. Experience with students has shown that they tend not to draw those finite distinctions. The section closes with a prototype for a windmill that could keep your students busy for several weeks and achieving amazing results.

Chapter 4 explores inclined planes and their variations, including double inclined planes, moving inclined planes, screws, and wedges. There are several opportunities for experimentation and extensions into mathematics.

Chapter 5 looks at friction. Questions about useful, rolling, and harmful friction are answered through experimentation. Reducing friction with lubricants, and increasing friction through pressure and surface area, are explored.

Mechanical advantage and how it relates to the various simple machines is the focus of chapter 6. The students will acquire intuitive as well as mathematical data relating to how simple machines help us do work.

I do really like to make bulletin boards, but it is nice for the students to be responsible for the construction, too. Ideas for bulletin boards and learning centers are provided in chapter 7.

The students need to demonstrate the level to which they have achieved as a result of your instruction. A hands-on final test is provided for your convenience in chapter 8.

Chapter 9 provides a glossary of lay definitions for you and your students' use. If you wish to develop vocabulary skill with your students you are welcome to duplicate it for your use. Definitions are provided for a few words that I made up to help with the explanation of some of the items you will be building and using.

HOW TO USE THIS BOOK

In keeping with the high-tech nature of this book and our society, it is important to explain how to use this book. Each of the activities is prefaced with the activity's main idea, a summary of the process skills students will be using, a list of materials needed, time allotted, and the procedure or steps used to perform the activity.

The Main Idea

In the world of educational jargon, terms like *concept, construct, generalization*, and so on, appear with great frequency and with an equal amount of casual exchangeability. Students acquire the main idea of an activity as a result of participation in the activity, which sounds a lot like an objective but is really a generalization because it is a group of concepts working together. This statement is not meant to confuse you, but rather to emphasize that the student should acquire one or two very simple generalizations (or whatever you want to call them) from each activity and be able to verbalize them when asked.

Process Skills

Measuring is one of a number of commonly agreed upon science process skills. Other process skills are identified, but throughout the activities only the following skills will be referenced:

Observing. Observation is the starting point for concept formation. The senses of sight, hearing, touch, taste, and smell are used to learn about objects and events.

Classifying. Identification of likenesses and differences for simple grouping leads to more complex categorizing and classifying based on relationships between objects and events.

Measuring. Exact measurements (e.g., length, area, volume, and temperature) are needed to describe and quantify objects and events.

Inferring. Inferring involves the proposing of interpretations, explanations, and causes from observed events and collected data.

Interpreting data. Interpretation is the explanation of information gathered by observations and investigations.

Predicting. Prediction of possible results or outcomes is based on observation and inferences.

Materials

The materials are the tools that are needed to do the job properly. Quantities listed refer to those needed by an individual or small group, not the entire class. You will need to multiply each item listed by the number of individuals or small groups that will be participating in the activity to get the right number of items needed for your group.

Time

All activities that are described have been used successfully with several groups of students within the time listed. However, your individual schedule will obviously influence the allocation of time for you.

Procedure

Each activity provides you with numbered steps to follow. If you progress with this manual in one hand and teach with the other, you will find your way to success.

STUDENT ASSESSMENT IN INTERACTIVE SCIENCE PROGRAMS

Evaluation within interactive science programs is a difficult and, to a certain extent, somewhat elusive task. Evaluation should be ongoing and criterion referenced. As always, it is most reliable when comprised of a collection of the results of a variety of instruments.

The following is a discussion of a variety of assessment tools that are useful for identifying students' growth as they participate in this unit of study. Elements of the assessment menu have been embedded in the unit. You may use these or develop your own as you see fit.

Activity Sheets

A variety of student activity sheets have been developed and included in this book. An activity sheet is an organized way of communicating predictions and observations. They are intended for your use, and you are encouraged to duplicate them. They are useful assessment tools in providing immediate feedback to you and your students. The responses or recorded data can easily be analyzed statistically for accuracy. When you use them for assessment, look for several things. First, do the predictions precede each observation? Are the predictions becoming more and more accurate? As students observe events, they should soon begin to observe patterns. These patterns then provide information to narrow the gap between anticipation and outcome. Note: Predictions are never judged as right or wrong; they are most important for investment in the outcome. I always give the students 100 percent on their predictions section if they make them. However, the predictions should not be used for statistical evaluation. The prediction is a thought process directed toward the outcome of cause and effect relationships. You should note the developmental process in the prediction, that is, look to see if the student is observing patterns and applying the information rather than guessing. By judging rightness or wrongness of the prediction, you will discourage the student from taking risks. Second, the observations should be accurate in relation to the event.

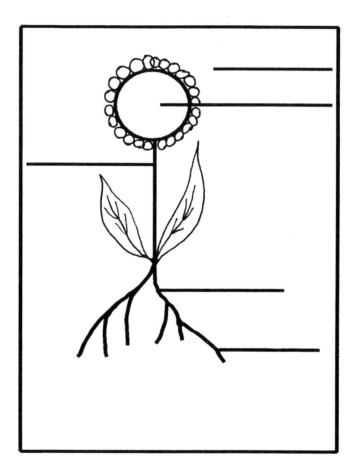

Pre- and Post-Drawings

The pre- and post-drawing format is a useful assessment tool. It will give you pertinent information about cognitive growth related to a selected representative element of the unit.

Drawings may be used for recording observations and for pre- and post-assessment. For observations, they are a valuable resource for determining student participation in activities. Drawings allow many students an opportunity to communicate observations they might not be able to express orally or through written description. When you use them for assessment purposes, look for 1) accuracy and 2) detail.

For pre- and post-assessment data, drawings are useful for assessment purposes. The student can be asked to draw an element from the unit. It is important that the element chosen be comfortable for most of the students (i.e., that they will have some prior knowledge of it). The subject of the drawing chosen should be addressed through some instruction in the unit. The summative (post-) drawing should reflect synthesis of information and processes acquired during their interactions. Compare the pre- and post-drawings and look for increases in content, detail, and accuracy.

USING THE PRE- AND POST-DRAWING FORM

Duplicate two copies of the pre- and post-drawing form for each student. Pass out one copy to the students at the onset of the unit. Ask them to write their name and date on the proper lines. Select a representative content sample from the unit

a. that you will be addressing through instruction;

b. with which you believe most students have some experience; and

c. with which most will achieve some level of success

and have the students fill in its name on the title line.

Discuss the expectations you have for the task with the students. You are looking to find what the students already know about the subject through what they show in the drawings and their labels. You will be comparing these drawings to ones they will be making at the end of the unit. For purposes of assessment, look for

a. growth in content;

b. degree of content in relation to the identified outcomes;

c. accuracy; and

d. how the drawing reflects synthesis of scientific content and processes.

For each of the criterion references rate the students individually according to the following system:

3—high
2—appropriate
1—low
0—not observable or not appropriate

It is appropriate to make annotated observations about a student's developmental ability in this particular assessment format as developmentally 1) advanced, 2) appropriate, or 3) delayed. Remember: The results of this instrument should be used in conjunction with the data from other products for your assessment of any student's progress.

Interviews

When you have the opportunity to discuss with individuals the progress they are making toward their goals, you can document and use the interchange as an assessment tool. Understandably, you will not be able to contact all or most students at any one time, but for validity, have a set of questions you could ask each student for any given activity. Check for the following:

1. level of understanding of content and process;

2. involvement; and

3. ability to apply what they have learned to new situations.

Journals

Today the word *journal* has a diversity of meanings, each relevant to the representatives of the disciplines with whom you talk. Historically, a journal is something in which someone wrote innermost thoughts without response from the reader. Now, in the world of whole language, the journal could be considered by some as a new name for a workbook or series of predetermined writing experiences.

For those outside of science, what is provided here might be considered a log. It is my experience that a log is a more detailed accounting of the actions of experimentation. Because neither the term *journal* nor *log* fits exactly for what is provided here, we are going to make an alphabetical decision and go with the word *journal.*

The intent of this journal is to provide a closure activity on a day-to-day basis for the experiments provided in this book. At the close of each activity ask the students to turn to their journals and complete the statement: "Today I learned...." A sample journal page is included in this section with procedures for its use. When the group has completed the activity, invite members of the group to share their responses. For student assessment, the journal entries should be evaluated in relation to overall conceptual development. You may additionally use the information for determining class progress. If a majority of the students don't reach consensus, consider what changes should be made to meet their needs.

Ideally, the journal page should be kept separate from the activity sheets. Doing this will make it an open-mind—not an open-page—experience. When filling in sheets like this there is a tendency for some students to key in on a word, number, or phrase and use that as the response if the activity sheet is at hand. When the sheet is not present, the student must invoke a thought process. The response is then a closure activity where the student is engaged in a "one more time" experience rather than fidgeting while *you* close the activity.

The data garnered from this activity are as valuable for determining how you did or how well the activity was received as they are assessing individual student growth. If the students individually are having difficulty, then you can address individual needs. But, if the group is having a hard time, then a little introspection might be necessary in relation to your delivery, the discussion of the results, or reinforcement and reteaching activities. Overwhelming enthusiasm might even encourage you to brave the world of extension activities. But be careful: We can't have them liking this science stuff.

Name————————————

——————————— **journal** ———————————

Date————— Today I learned: ————————————

—————— ——————————————————————
—————— ——————————————————————
—————— ——————————————————————
—————— ——————————————————————
—————— ——————————————————————
—————— ——————————————————————
—————— ——————————————————————
—————— ——————————————————————
—————— ——————————————————————
—————— ——————————————————————
—————— ——————————————————————
—————— ——————————————————————
—————— ——————————————————————
—————— ——————————————————————
—————— ——————————————————————
—————— ——————————————————————
—————— ——————————————————————
—————— ——————————————————————
—————— ——————————————————————
—————— ——————————————————————
—————— ——————————————————————
—————— ——————————————————————
—————— ——————————————————————

Observations

The included observation form is provided for your use as part of the assessment options for your science program. With some practice and growing familiarity of the form, it should provide you with valuable data to collate with other input as you develop an academic profile for each of your students. Adapt it to best fit your needs. Use the form as follows:

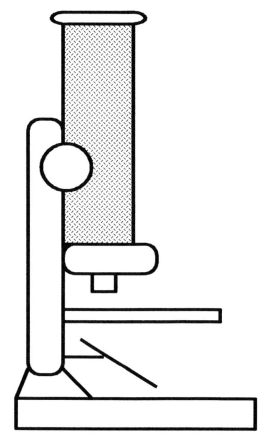

a. Enter the student's name once, then photocopy the form several times for multiple uses.

b. Place numerical entry of the month, day, and year in the "DATE" column for future reference.

c. Place a check mark to indicate the type of experience with which the student is involved or identify the specific task in the "OTHER" column. Rate the student with one of the following:

   3 — high
   2 — appropriate
   1 — low
   0 — not observable or not applicable

Observations may be carried out by the teacher while students are engaged in an activity. For assessment purposes the observer should be looking for the following:

Engagement — student actively addresses the task at hand in a scientific manner.

Process skill application — student demonstrates an ability to apply the identified skill of measurement, classification, observation, interpretation, inference, or prediction.

Content development — student demonstrates understanding of scientific content and generalizations.

Cooperation — student assumes one or more of the collective roles in a group activity.

Problem-solving skills — student applies problem-solving strategies appropriate to the activity.

Efficiency — student plans and uses time effectively while conducting scientific procedures in relation to the task at hand.

The form should be simple and easy to use as the observer will only be able to commit short periods of time to the process. Try to observe all students in a similar format. A section for annotated comments is provided for your convenience to document other pertinent observations. Remember: Use the results of this instrument in conjunction with the data from other products for your assessment of any student's progress.

OBSERVATION FORM

DATE	STUDENT	TYPE OF ACTIVITY			Engagement	Process Skills	Content	Cooperation	Problem Solving	Efficiency	Other
		EXPERIMENT	GROUP PROJECT	OTHER							

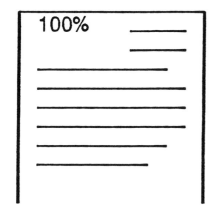

Pretests/Posttests

Pretests and posttests are assessment tools that can provide useful data. On an individual basis they can be brainstorming, drawings (described earlier), laboratory reports, and paper-and-pencil tests.

a. *Brainstorming activities* ask students to list all the related things they can about the unit or element of the unit at the onset and again at the close.

b. *Drawing* a representation of some significant event at the beginning and end of a science activity is revealing.

c. A *laboratory report* is the resulting product from the formation of a hypothesis and the ensuing original experimental design and setup. The description of the design and student interpretation of the results is useful for assessment purposes.

d. *Paper-and-pencil tests* ask the student to share information about unit content. The tests can ask for information, to choose or select a correct response from pictorial representations, or to select from a series of options. Alternate forms should be provided.

Products—Post Unit

This genre of assessment tools provides the students the opportunity to synthesize the learnings of the unit.

a. *Demonstrations/projects.* The student has the opportunity to prepare a visual representation for a suggested or self-generated topic. Assessment should be based on predesigned criteria addressing scientific principles as well as quality of presentation.

b. *Designing experiments.* To assess growth students should be encouraged to design, conduct, and report on experiments. Assessment should reference design and procedural components.

c. *Visual and performing arts.* A viable alternative for assessment can come from visual and performing arts. Through skits, plays, songs, graphics, and so on, students can provide summative data. Evaluation should relate to scientific content and processes depicted.

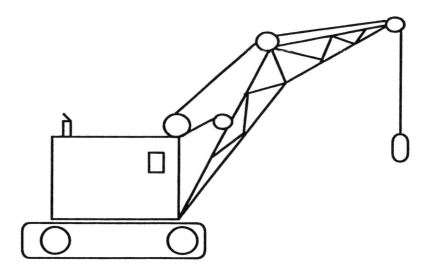

Troubleshooting

This is a situational assessment tool. It asks the student to analyze a situational problem to determine the cause-effect relation observed. The experience could be any one of the following:

a. a written response to a described situation;

b. an oral or written response to a pictorial representation; or

c. a tactile problem with a written, oral, or representational response.

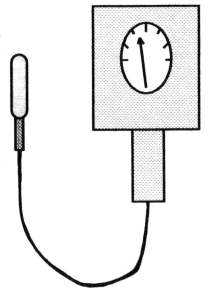

Writing, Pre- and Post-

Comparative data are provided in the writing situation. The students are asked to share what they currently know about the content of the unit or a significant part by responding to parallel questions, for example, "What do you know about levers?" and "What do you know about levers now?"

Unquestionably, there are many options for assessment that will accommodate a variety of teaching styles. Your professional judgment can best determine which tools to select, though it is imperative that the assessment be tailored to the uniqueness of the students' experiences.

As you weave the assessment fabric, keep in mind that effective assessment has several requirements. Student performance is most representative if the assessment occurs in a natural setting to reduce the stress always incurred by students. Assessment is a matrix of data collated from multiple sources. Finally, it should assess growth through the selection of elements from the unit and sampling at the onset and at the close of the unit.

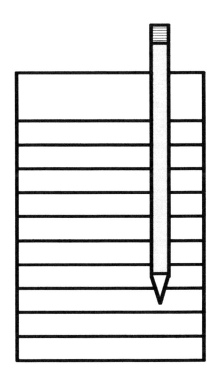

1
TOOLS OF THE TRADE

Are you convinced yet? You know, about simple machines being simple? Now that it is getting down to the time that you are starting to think about using some of these activities with students, the materials dilemma jumps up and bites you in the leg. This section should ease some of the tension by starting the students and you off on the road to success. At least I was sure of it until I got off the plane in Houston. Perhaps I should explain....

In March of 1991, I was accepted to do a presentation on this very topic for the National Science Teachers Conference. After much planning, copying, and packing, I was ready to venture off into a part of the world that I had never seen before. With me was everything that is really important for teaching science: rulers, masking tape, and paper clips ... lots of paper clips. In an hour we were to make spring scales, levers, and masses, as well as do a few experiments. All that was needed for the session was a couple hundred rocks about the size of a student's fist. Nothing to it, right? The day before the session, I started to do a little scouting out and about to snatch a bucketful of rocks from along the side of the road. Needless to say, this young lad from the Pacific Northwest was in for an unpleasant surprise in Houston (actually, just one of several).

Of course, all good science teachers are problem solvers. So, it was off to the Information Booth to find out where a person would be able to go find a few rocks. An hour and 26 "someone here must knows" later, I was no closer to having any rocks or a workshop. This is starting to sound a lot like a science lesson, isn't it? The resolution to the problem didn't come from the trip to the construction site just a few miles down the road. It actually came from a bunch of us poor lost waifs wandering around in a parking lot in the dark of night picking up chunks of broken-up concrete.

The descriptions that follow will help you and your students to make some very essential, and for the most part much more durable, pieces of scientific equipment for use in the activities described in this book. You will be making a mass, spring scale, lever, and pulley. These items can be purchased if you so choose, but in my experience the real value is in the students being involved in their construction. All you will need is a rock; a ruler or thin, narrow board; masking tape; paper clips; rubber bands; a wire clothes hanger; empty thread spools; and just a dash of patience.

masses

MAIN IDEA: Here is how to make a handy mass for use in activities that follow.

MATERIALS:

Jumbo paper clips (1 per student)
Masking tape
Stones (1 per student, about the size of their fist)

TIME: 30 minutes

PROCEDURE:

1. Lay a paper clip flat on the table. (Hint: If you demonstrate this on the overhead projector it really helps the students.) Open the inside loop out as you would open a book until it forms the letter *C*. If you do this properly, the paper clip will not break. If it forms the letter *S*, the wire twists, fatigues, and usually breaks.

2. Slide the end of an 18-inch piece of masking tape through the largest loop of the paper clip, then wrap the remainder of the tape around the stone and the paper clip until you run out of tape.

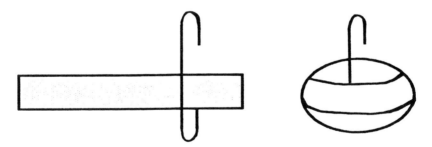

Your mass is now ready for use in a lot of the exercises that follow. If you are lifting the mass, bend the exposed hook of the paper clip upward so it is easier to attach. If you pull the mass along, as in a test for friction, then flatten the hook out.

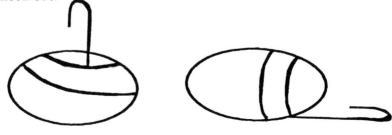

making a spring scale

MAIN IDEA: Phenomena are measurable.

A spring scale is a useful tool for *measuring*.

PROCESS SKILL: Measuring

MATERIALS:

Jumbo paper clips (1 per student)
Masking tape
Rubber bands
Wooden rulers or pieces of plywood (1/4 by 1 by 12 inches)

TIME: 30-45 minutes

Students may work alone or in pairs.

PROCEDURE:

1. Pass out the rulers, paper clips, and 2 pieces of masking tape to each student. One piece should be about 4 inches long, the second should be about 12 inches long.

2. Have the students cover the length of one side of the ruler or plywood with the longest piece of tape.

3. If they cover a ruler they should be able to see the increments on the ruler through the tape. Have them mark the tape every 1/4 inch or centimeter, whichever you prefer. *Do not number the marks yet!* If you use plywood strips, lay a ruler parallel to the taped surface and mark the increments every 1/4 inch or centimeter.

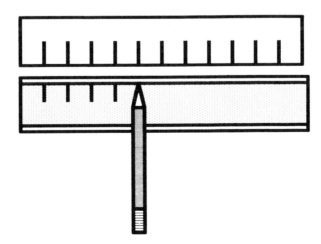

4. Place the paper clip on a table. Holding the larger loop down firmly, hook your fingernail under the smaller loop and bend it up slightly.

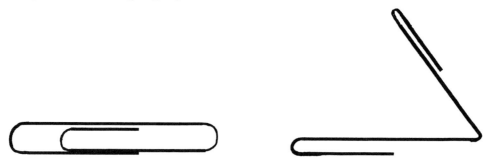

5. Slide the rubber band over the small loop of the paper clip.

6. Slip the paper clip and rubber band over either end of the ruler so that the rubber band lays along the side of the spring scale with the tape and the marks.

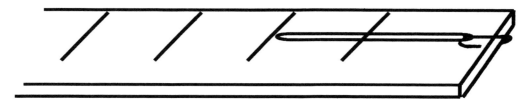

7. Take about 4 inches of tape and wrap it around the end of the ruler, trapping the paper clip and the rubber band.

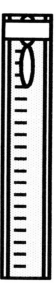

8. With the point of a pencil, gently stretch the rubber band so that all the slack is removed, but that the rubber band is not being stretched. Label the closest mark on the tape "0," then number each mark sequentially away from the rubber band until you reach the end of the spring scale.

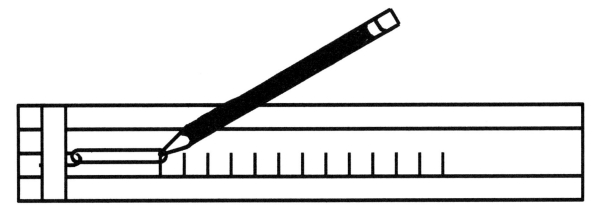

The units of the spring scale are standard, but not customary. This means that each of the marks has the same value, but the marks themselves do not relate to any known unit.

This is a handy little device because any time a rubber band breaks, all you have to do is unwrap the tape, put on a new one, and away you go. Also, there is a wide range of scales that you can use. If you are in need of a heavy-duty machine, put on a heavy band. If a light touch is the order of the day, then put on a lighter band.

using the spring scale

MAIN IDEA: A spring scale may be used to measure the amount of force it takes to do a job.

A spring scale will also measure the weight of an object.

The spring scale will measure in standard units.

PROCESS SKILL: Measuring

MATERIALS:
Masses
Spring scales

TIME: 10 minutes

PROCEDURE:

1. If you have used a commercial spring scale before, you know that you pulled to apply force. With this spring scale you will be lifting or pushing in order to stretch the rubber band enough to apply force.

2. The units of measurement will be standard with each one being worth the same amount; however, they will not be customary. Customary units are calibrated to a known measure such as grams or ounces. Students can deal very easily with this concept, though at first they will try and assign unit values other than just "units."

3. *Point of reference* is going to be a very important concept to get across to the students at this point. When you calibrated the units on the spring scale, you gently stretched the rubber band so that there was no slack in it. From the end of the rubber band, or point of reference, the marks on the spring scale were numbered. As force is added to the rubber band, it will stretch. The students should watch the end of the rubber band to determine how much force is being added to the rubber band for purposes of measurement.

4. To teach the students to read the units, take the point of a ballpoint pen or pencil, and hook it in the loop of the spring scale. Stretch it to the number "5." Ask "How much force is being applied to the spring scale?" The response should be "5." Pretty simple, right? Keep adding force and inquiring as to the reading on the scale.

5. Now try weighing an actual object (see page 7). Direct the students to grasp the spring scale so the "0" is held straight up and they can see the numbers on the tape. Then, have them hook their mass to the spring scale and gently release it so the rubber band stretches and comes to rest. Remembering that the end of the rubber band is the point of reference, ask them to share the weight of their masses. To extend the practice, have the students trade masses. Even using the rubber band spring scales, you will find an amazing consistency in the weights of any particular mass.

From *Simple Machines Made Simple.* Copyright © 1993. Teacher Ideas Press, P.O. Box 6633, Englewood, CO 80155-6633.

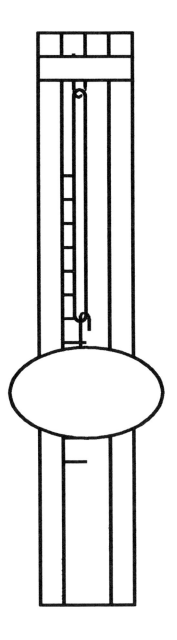

making a lever

MAIN IDEA: A lever is a bar or rod that turns on a point called a fulcrum.

A lever is a simple machine.

PROCESS SKILL: Measuring

MATERIALS:

Jumbo paper clips (1 per student)
Masking tape
Wooden rulers or pieces of 1/4-inch plywood cut 1 by 12-1/2 inches

TIME: 30 minutes

PROCEDURE:

1. Pass out paper clips, wooden rulers, and about 12 inches of masking tape to each student.

2. Cover one side of the plywood strip or the numbered side of the wooden ruler with the masking tape.

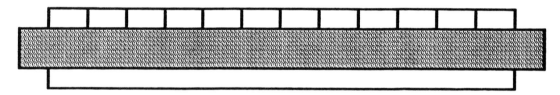

3. Place a ruler along the lever and place marks on the tape every inch.

4. If you used a wooden ruler for the lever, then place a "1" on the first mark and then number to "12," with "12" at the end of the lever. If you use the plywood strips, then the mark 1/2 inch from the end of the lever is "0" and you will number sequentially to "12" at the end of the lever.

5. Lay the paper clip on the table. While holding it down, reach in and hook the inside loop. Pull the inside loop up to a right angle.

6. Lay the paper clip on the end of the lever marked "12" so that the larger loop is on the tape and the smaller loop is extended below the lever (see page 9).

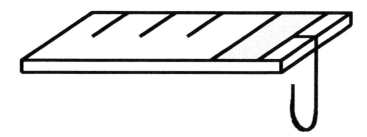

7. Tape the large loop in place with masking tape. The tape should be snug, but not tight. You now have a handy first- and third-class lever for use in experiments.

    To change the lever for second-class lever experiments, where the force is applied in an upward direction, all you have to do is rotate the smaller loop up so that it is on the same side as the tape. You will find that if the tape is not too tight, the whole clip will turn and not fatigue the wire of the clip, causing it to break.

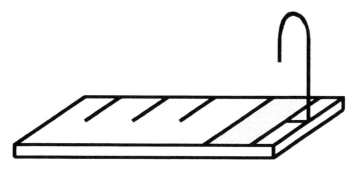

making a pulley

MAIN IDEA: A pulley is a form of a wheel and axle where the outer edge of the wheel has a groove.

A pulley is a simple machine.

PROCESS SKILL: Measuring

MATERIALS:
Masking tape
Thread spools
Wire clothes hangers
Wire cutters

TIME: 30-45 minutes

PROCEDURE:
At some point previous to conducting the activity, have the students start collecting empty thread spools and wire clothes hangers.

1. Pass out one wire hanger and thread spool to each student.

2. Clip off the base of the hanger.

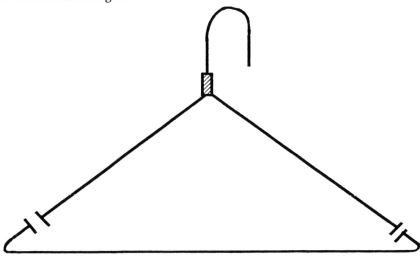

3. Bend the 2 legs of the hanger straight out.

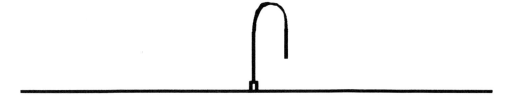

---

4. Place the spool on the table so the center of the spool lines up with the center of the wire hanger. Allow a little room on each side of the spool and bend the wires straight down along the ends of the spool.

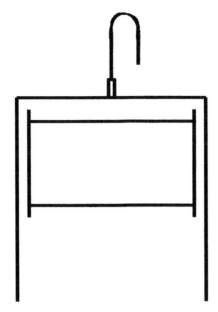

5. Bend 1 wire straight in at a right angle.

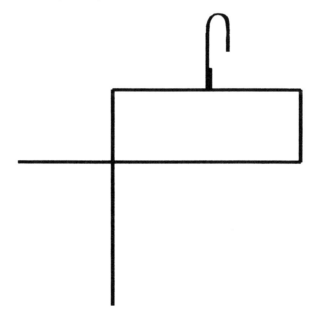

6. Slide the spool over the wire.

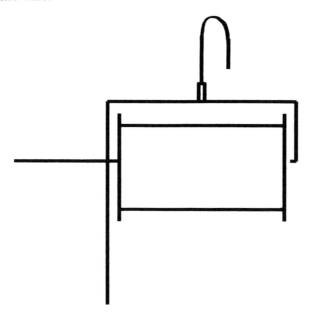

7. Bend the cross wire straight up alongside of the second leg. Tape the 2 wires together with a short piece of masking tape.

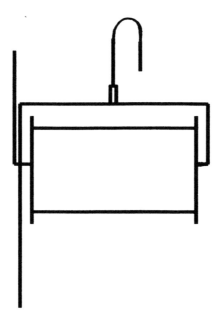

8. Clip off only the extra piece of the upper wire.

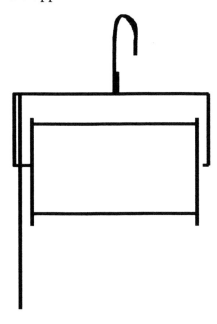

9. Now you have two choices. If you want to use this only as a single pulley, trim off all of the lower wire (a). If you want to use the pulley as part of a block and tackle, bend the lower wire inward a short distance below the spool. At the center line of the spool, bend a short loop and clip off the extra (b).

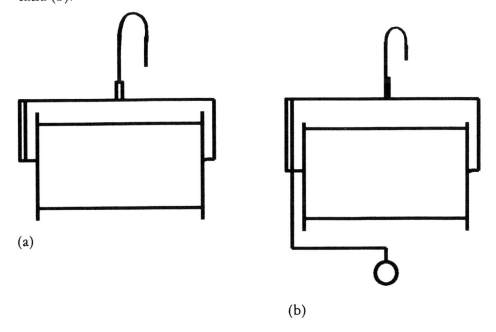

(a)

(b)

□
2
THINGS THAT PIVOT

lev′er (lev′r; lev′ar) n. 1. a bar resting on and tending to rotate about a fixed point, the fulcrum, when force is applied at one end.

The lever is one of the simple machines. It is a bar or rod that turns on a point known as the fulcrum. However, the dictionary definition is not complete.

There are four components of the lever system. The bar or rod is the lever. The lever is usually longer than it is wide or thick, though not always, as in the case of the handle of a light switch. The lever must pivot or turn on a point, known as the fulcrum, to do its work. The force is applied to the lever to move an object or the load.

The dictionary definition falls short because the force is not always applied to the end of the lever. How the components are arranged determines the class of the lever. Because there are three ways the fulcrum, force, and load may be arranged about the lever, there are three classes of levers. The component that is in the middle determines the class of the lever.

The first-class lever is the most common. The image it brings to mind is that of a teeter-totter or seesaw. It is almost always the only image students have. In a first-class lever the fulcrum is always positioned in the middle, and the load and force are located at opposite ends (i.e., the dictionary definition). The force always moves in the opposite direction of the load, and the lever gains its mechanical advantage as the fulcrum is located closer to the load.

In a second-class lever the load is located in the middle and the force and fulcrum are located at opposite ends. The force and the load always move in the same direction. The lever gains in mechanical advantage as the load and fulcrum get closer together, much the same as the first-class lever. Some common examples of second-class levers are wrenches, nutcrackers, wheelbarrows, and the handle of a pencil sharpener.

The third-class lever locates the force in the middle and the fulcrum and load at opposite ends. The force and load always move in the same direction, but unlike the second-class lever, the force can never travel farther than the load, therefore, there is never any positive mechanical advantage. Common third-class levers are our arms and legs, fishing poles, cranes, and backhoes.

Right now you are probably at the unnnnnnnnnnnnnnnnh! stage of simple machines. You've been here before and didn't like it. Well, I can only encourage you to try the lever-related activities that follow, complete with anticipatory sets, student activity sheets ready for duplication, and application activities. We are working under the assumption that the research on the learning cycle is valid and that we need to see something at least three times before there is any hope of retaining it. Because most of us are learning science as we teach it, now is a good time to begin learning. The information about levers will be revisited as you conduct the activities and review the discussions of the results that follow the activities.

draw me

Name_____

Date_____

Draw several different kinds of levers in action.

the floating hammer

MAIN IDEA: A first-class lever will remain in balance when the load is evenly distributed on either side of the fulcrum.

PROCESS SKILLS: Inferring
Interpreting data
Observing

MATERIALS:
12-inch ruler
8 inches of string tied in a loop
Hammer

TIME: 10 minutes

This demonstration is very useful as an anticipatory set for the "first-class levers" activity to follow.

PROCEDURE:

1. Begin by showing the students the materials you will be using. Showmanship can help if you explain that they will need to learn some "scientific words" to take an active part in this activity. Have them repeat the words *hammer, string,* and *ruler* after you, one at a time.

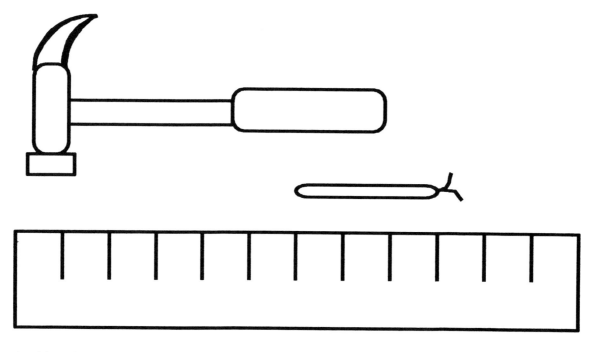

2. At this point they obviously won't be very impressed! Assemble the parts as shown. A little practice before you demonstrate is always a good idea (see page 17).

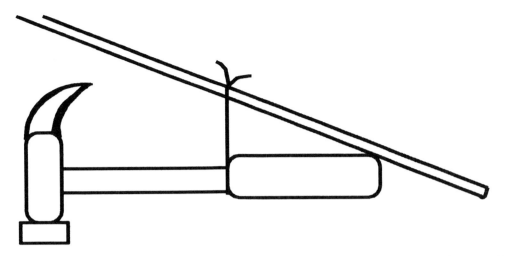

3. You probably still don't have their attention. However, they will soon start to show interest if you balance the system on the end of your index finger. The balance point is the end of the ruler above the head of the hammer. Minor experimentation will probably need to be made here as each system is slightly different, depending on the length of the loop of string, the exact positioning of the string, and the weight of the hammer you choose. Moving the string along the ruler changes the distribution of the weight and the balance.

4. For the coup de grâce, balance the system on the projecting lens of your overhead projector, the pull-down handle of your projection screen, or the edge of a bookshelf or table.

5. Demonstrate how solid the balance is by tapping the end of the ruler, causing the system to rock as a teeter-totter.

Remember the "Main Idea." If the load is the same on either side of the fulcrum, the lever will remain in balance. The point on which the ruler is balancing is the fulcrum. If you draw an imaginary line straight down from the fulcrum, you should be able to visualize that about an equal amount of mass lies on either side of the fulcrum. After the students conduct the "first-class levers" activity, see if they can explain this event.

first-class levers

MAIN IDEA: A lever is first-class if the fulcrum is located between the mass and force.

A first-class lever helps us do work by trading force for distance.

PROCESS SKILLS: Interpreting data
Measuring
Predicting

MATERIALS:
Lever
Masking tape
Mass
Pencil (for fulcrum)
Spring scale

TIME: 45 minutes

It works well if students cooperate as pairs.

PROCEDURE:

1. Demonstrate how to set up the experiment.

    a. Place a pencil near and parallel to the edge of a table.

    b. Lay the lever perpendicular to the fulcrum, with the hook pointing in a downward direction out over the edge of the table.

    c. Use about 2 inches of tape and curl it into a circle with the sticky side out.

    d. Attach the tape to the "0" end of the lever and place the mass on the tape.

    e. Hook the rubber band of the spring scale to the lever so that the spring scale will exert pressure in a downward direction (see top of page 19).

2. Now is a good time to introduce the students to the idea of *fulcrum distance*, the distance between the fulcrum and the mass. This is the variable to be manipulated in the experiment. If the mass is located at 0 inches and the fulcrum is located at 2 inches, the fulcrum distance would be 2 inches.

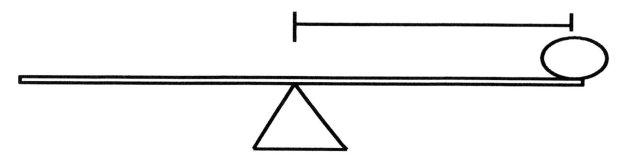

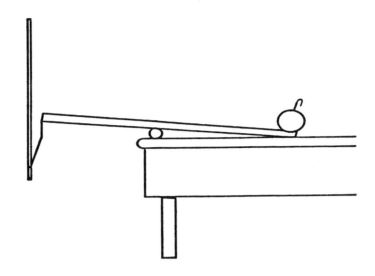

3. To make sure the students know how to set up the experiment, ask one of the students to demonstrate the setup for the group.

4. Working in pairs, have the students weigh their masses and enter the weight on the activity sheet.
    "My mass weighs _____ units."

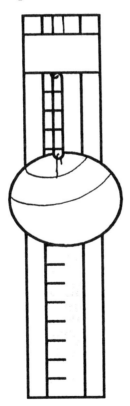

5. You're about ready to begin! The students should test how much force it takes to lift the mass with fulcrum distances of 2 inches, 4 inches, 6 inches, 8 inches, and 10 inches, recording the results after each trial.

NAME _____

DATE _____

——————————— first-class levers ———————————

1. Use your spring scale to find the weight of your mass. Remember that to apply force you must push up. Look at the end of the rubber band for your point of reference.

    "My mass weighs _____ units."

2. Set up your experiment so that the fulcrum distance is 2 inches. Predict how much force it will take to lift your mass and write your prediction in the chart.

3. Try it out! How much force did it really take? Were you close? Record the information on the chart.

4. Now continue the pattern. Add 2 inches to the fulcrum distance, predict how much force it will take, and try it out and record the results.

Trial	Fulcrum distance	Predicted force	Actual force
1			
2			
3			
4			
5			

5. Graph the results on the next page.

6. From the graph, see if you can figure out when there is no more mechanical advantage. The fulcrum distance was about _____ inches when it didn't help me any more.

GRAPHING THE RESULTS

To graph the results of the following lever experiments we will be using a broken-line graph. Depending on the grade level of your students, they might or might not have had much experience with the process; however by grade two, many have seen X,Y coordinates in some fashion, especially with the game "Battleship."

1. Label the grid sheet with the appropriate class of lever.

2. Have the students transfer the fulcrum distance and force information from the appropriate activity sheet to the grid sheet. (A graph is a record of results plotted on a grid.)

3. The fulcrum distances have been labeled for you, but the force axis hasn't been. The reason is that until the experiment has been conducted and you know the range of force readings, you don't know how big to make the increments. If the range of force readings is small, it doesn't make much sense to number by 10s; inversely, if the force readings are high you wouldn't want to use 1s. So, if the top readings are in the 20s, then number by 1s; if they are in the 40s, by 2s; if they are in the 60s, by 3s; and so on.

4. Demonstrate how to do the numbering; an overhead transparency of the grid sheet is helpful.

5. Plot a horizontal line for the weight of the mass. This is a reference point for later discussion. If the force necessary to lift the mass is below this line, there is positive mechanical advantage (it takes less force to lift the mass than if you picked it up with your hand). When the graph passes above the horizontal line, then there is negative mechanical advantage or it takes more force to lift the mass than if you were to pick it up with your hand.

6. Plot the fulcrum distance/force readings and connect the points to complete the graphing.

7. Use the results of the graphing to discuss the advantages and disadvantages of using the lever.

graphing the results

Lever class_____   Name_____
                                 Date_____

1. Transfer the data from your activity sheet to the table below
2. Draw a horizontal line at the weight of the mass
3. Locate your coordinates (points)
4. Connect the points with a "broken" line

Weight of the mass	units						
Fulcrum distance							
Force							

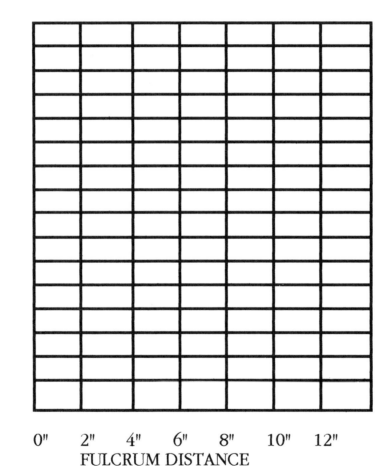

F
O
R
C
E

0"   2"   4"   6"   8"   10"   12"
FULCRUM DISTANCE

INTERPRETING THE GRAPHS

Now that you have made the graphs, what do they mean? Let's look at the three classes of levers, one at a time.

With the *first-class lever* you will notice that about half of the graph is above the heavy horizontal line and half is below. Remember that the horizontal line indicates the weight of the mass or the amount of the force that it would take to lift something with your hand, unaided by a machine. When the machine is not helping you from a force standpoint, you are not trading force for distance. Note, however, that this might be desirable at times. The first-class lever serves two purposes. One, it allows you to trade force for distance, and two, it reverses the direction in which force is applied. For example, it doesn't take much force to flip a light switch, a first-class lever in most cases. The little handle allows you to activate and protect the delicate mechanism by reversing the direction of force and reducing the amount of force by the location of the fulcrum.

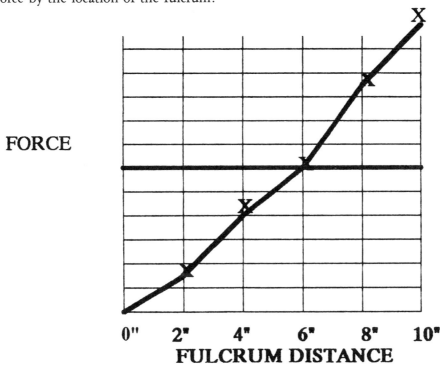

Probably the most important generalization that one can make about this lever system is that the closer the fulcrum is to the mass or load, the easier it is to lift. A humorous aside is worth sharing here: One of my favorite hobbies is fishing. I use a trailerable boat, the combination of which weighs about 1,500 pounds. One of the trailer tires had a slow leak, with the air lasting about eight days without the tire going flat. So, this was a perfect excuse to go fishing every weekend, right? ("Oops, honey, the trailer tire needs some air.") Circumstances required me to miss a week, so I was faced with taking the tire in to be fixed. The problem was that boat trailers are built close to the ground, and with a flat tire it is impossible to place the jack under the frame. So I enlisted the aid of my son to place the jack under the frame at just the right moment. Selecting a perfect board and rock, I assembled a lever with the fulcrum close to the trailer, but now the end of the 12-foot board was 10 feet above the ground. I still visualize the picture of me climbing up a step ladder to get to the end of the lever so I could grab the lever and work my way back down the ladder. The net effect was that I was able to lift the boat and trailer off the ground just far enough to slide the jack under the frame (see page 24). What some people won't do to go fishing!

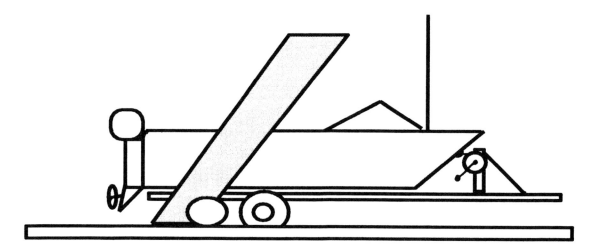

a simple balance

MAIN IDEA: A single-beam balance is a useful application of a first-class lever.

PROCESS SKILLS: Interpreting data
Measuring
Observing

MATERIALS:
2 4-ounce cups for each student
12-inch ruler or pegboard
Modeling clay
String
Wire hanger

TIME: 45 minutes

This activity has been used very nicely with groups of about 25 first graders.

PROCEDURE:
1. You may use a plastic or wooden ruler with 3 holes in it (the kind students like to pretend are helicopter rotors), Or cut sheets of utility pegboard into strips about 1 inch wide by 12 inches long. (Pegboard is available in 4-by-8-foot sheets. Many rulers come with 3 holes in them to fit nicely into students' 3-ring binders. Either is a good option.) If you use the pegboard, cut it so that there are an odd number of holes on each strip.

2. Punch 2 holes opposite each other near the rim of each cup. Cut 2 pieces of string about 4 to 6 inches long.

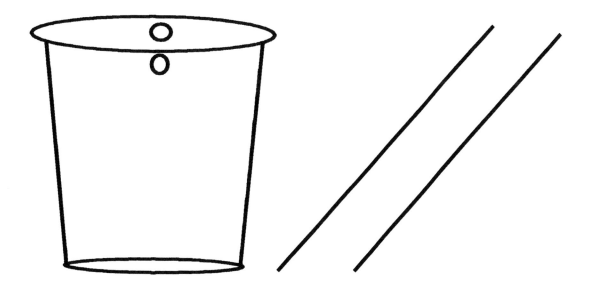

3. Grasp the hook of the wire hanger. You are going to be making 2 bends. First, twist the hook at a 90-degree angle to the rest of the hanger. Then, bend the hook straight back at a 90-degree angle from the frame of the hanger.

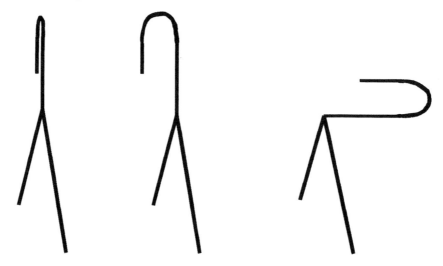

4. Now hold the hanger by the two lower corners of the frame so the hook is pointing toward your body. Bend the two lower corners toward each other until they will stay about 6 inches apart. This is the frame of your balance. Set it aside for a few minutes.

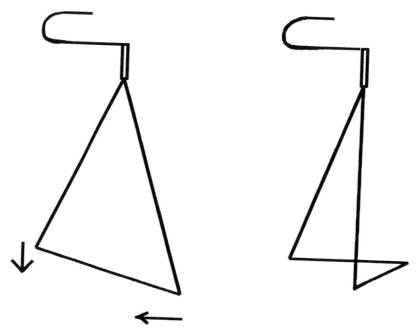

5. Tie one end of one of the pieces of string to a hole in the top of a cup. Feed the loose end through one end hole in the ruler or pegboard. Tie the loose end to the other hole in the cup. Repeat the process for the other cup, feeding the end of the string through the hole on the opposite end of the ruler or pegboard (see page 27).

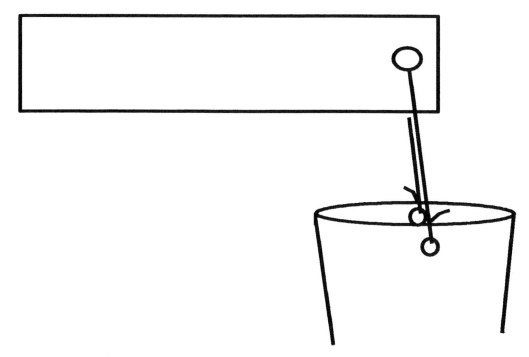

6. Slide the center hole of the ruler or pegboard over the hook on the hanger frame. Your balance is nearly ready to use. To true your balance, just put little dabs of clay in one of the cups until the bar is level. Remember, always add weight to the side that is the highest. You are now ready to do some easy balancing or first-class lever activities.

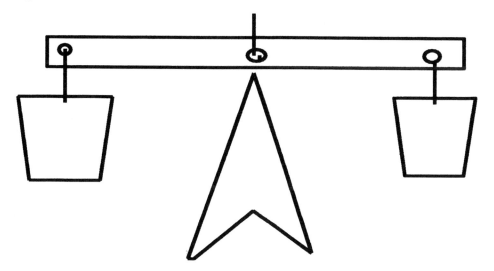

standard but not customary

MAIN IDEA: Measurement of weight requires standard units, though they may not be the ones with which we are familiar.

PROCESS SKILLS: Classifying
Interpreting data
Observing
Predicting

MATERIALS:
1 balance per student or group
Quantities of items that are fairly standard, for example, tacks, paper clips, beans, washers, or pennies
Objects to weigh such as an eraser, pencil, stone, chalk, or paper

TIME: 45 minutes

PROCEDURE:

1. Using the balances you just constructed, make sure they are even (in balance). Sometimes the process of storing or moving the balances will throw things off a little. The balancing is easily accomplished by adding to or removing a little modeling clay from the cup.

2. Distribute the standard units to the groups of students.

3. The standardization process can be done in two ways. The first is to place 1 unit (a paper clip unit) in the left-hand cup. Then, in the right-hand cup place another similar unit to check to see if they are the same. You will be surprised at the number that are quite different even though they appear to be identical. Make piles of standardized units.

   The second method is to try to find standard batches of paper clip units. Place batches of 5 units in each cup. If the batches are similar (exact is really hard to come by), then the units can be considered to be standard.

4. The next step is to develop a system of graded units (scientifically called masses). Pass out the other standard units that you will be using. Ask the students to predict what the order of the units will be from lightest to heaviest by placing a sample of each of the units in order from left to right on the table. They may verify their prediction in two ways, first by hefting them in their hands, then by placing the units in their balances.

5. Now that the order has been verified, the students need to find out the actual increment sizes (i.e., 1 paper clip unit is equal to 3 tack units or 6 bean units). Obviously, the product size is going to make a lot of difference. Jumbo paper clips are going to be quite a bit heavier than #3 clips, and lima beans are going to be a lot heavier than lentils.

6. As a mathematics extension, the students could graph the results of their standard noncustomary mass system using bar graphs or pictographs.

---

machine mobiles

MAIN IDEA: A first-class lever is in balance when the load is equal on either side of the fulcrum.

PROCESS SKILLS: Interpreting data
Measuring
Predicting

MATERIALS:
Clear tape
Crayons
Pictures of models of machines
Tagboard
Thread
Wire cutters
Wire hangers (1 per student)

TIME: 1 hour or more

This is an excellent cooperative learning activity as there is need of assistance when it comes to the tying of the thread to the wire and balancing of the mobile.

Prior to the activity, ask the students to each bring in a wire hanger.

PROCEDURE:

1. Have the students draw, cut out, and color 4 machines on their tagboard. Things like wheelbarrows and bicycles work well, although if you want to build the mobiles using the principles of levers and balance to support another theme, like favorite storybook characters, that is perfectly scientific as well. Just remember to discuss with them the scientific principles you are applying.

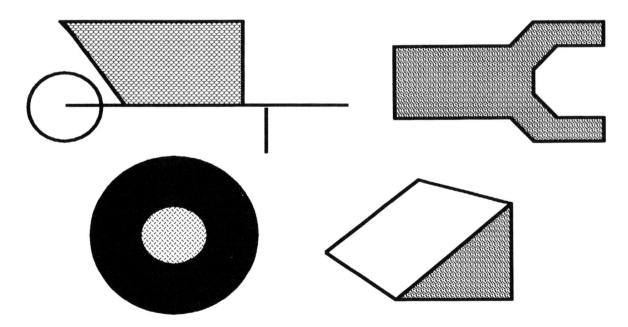

2. While they are designing the 4 models, go around and cut the hangers into 3 pieces—1 short, 1 medium, and 1 long straight piece. Dispose of the rest.

3. When the students have finished with the models, they can begin construction of the mobile. First, tape 6 to 8 inches of thread to the approximate top and middle of each model.

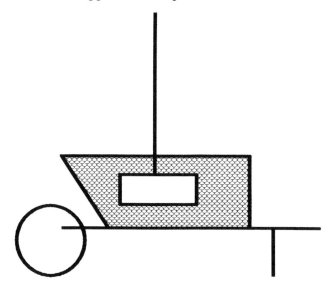

4. Next, sort the models into 1 group of 2 and 2 groups of 1. You are now ready to begin assembly. Take the 2 models and tie one to each end of the shortest wire.

5. Now tie 1 remaining model to 1 end of each of the remaining wires.

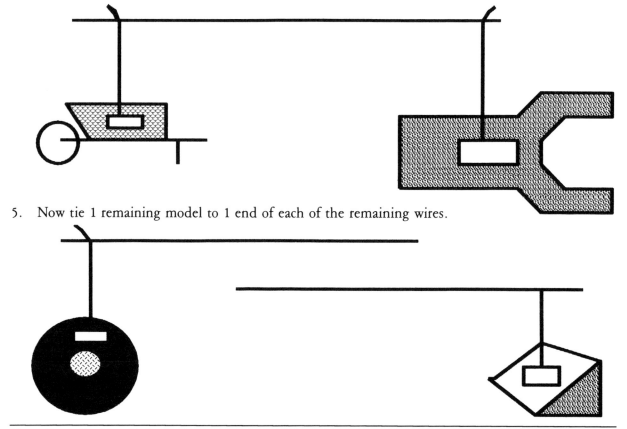

6. Assemble the mobile from the bottom up. Each student will need 3 more pieces of thread 6 to 12 inches long. Tie one of the pieces of thread to the point they "predict" the shortest wire will balance. When tying this series of knots to the wires, wrap the thread about 3 times around the wire before making a double knot. It will save a tremendous amount of frustration later. Hold the short wire and 2 models up by the thread and see if the wire balances. Slide the knot back and forth until it does. This is a good time to get the students to generalize about how to move the knot (always toward the heavy end!).

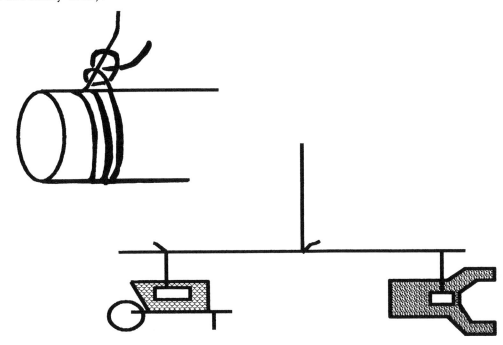

7. When this part is in balance, twist the loose end of the thread around the free end of the middle-length wire and tie it tightly. Then take another loose piece of thread, predict the balance point (balancing it on the tip of the index finger often helps), and then tie the end tightly.

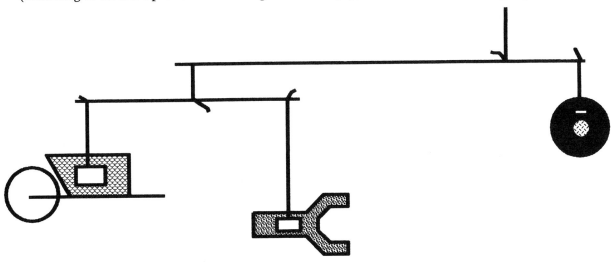

8. When this system is in balance, twist the end of the thread around the free end of the longest wire and tie it tightly. Take the last piece of the thread, predict the balance point of the longest wire, and tie it in place. Balance the whole system now.

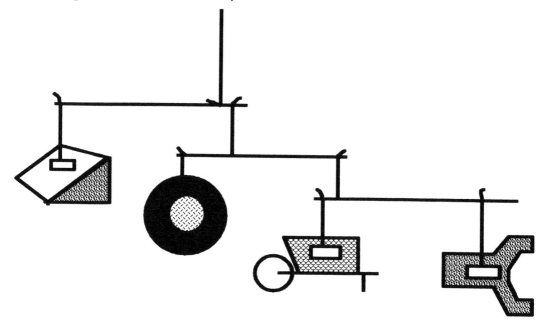

9. This would be a good time to work in pairs as one person holds the main thread and the other balances the parts. Always start from the bottom up! If problems arise from knots sliding along the wires, isolate one section, balance it, then put a very small piece of clear tape over the knot and wire to hold it in place. Then work your way up the mobile.

10. Congratulations on your work! Suspend it from the ceiling for all to admire.

the missing dot

MAIN IDEA: A second-class lever has the mass located between the force and the fulcrum.

PROCESS SKILLS: Inferring
Predicting

MATERIALS:
1 cutout of the letters *E, F,* and *M*
Overhead projector

TIME: 10 minutes

This is a good anticipatory set for the "second-class levers" activity that follows. The letters stand for:

E = Energy/Force (to avoid confusion with the fulcrum)
F = Fulcrum
M = Mass

PROCEDURE:

1. Ask the students if they have ever seen the trick where a pea is hidden under one of three shells, the shells are mixed up, and someone has to guess under which shell the pea is hidden. Explain that what you will be doing will be very similar.

2. Turn on the overhead projector and place the three letters on the screen. They will be able to see black letter shapes. Dramatically show the backs of each of the three letters to prove to them that there is nothing on the back of each. Then, with a colored pen, make a dot on the back of the *M*.

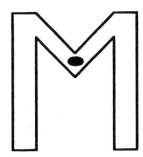

3. Place the *M* with the dot facing down and mix the letters thoroughly.

4. END WITH THE *M* IN THE MIDDLE!

5. Ask the students to predict under which letter the dot is now located. Most will not be fooled, of course, but their attention is now on the combination of letters. Show them where the dot is, revealing the *M* last.

6. Discuss with them the new combination of letters in relation to lever systems. Place a pencil on the screen to act as a lever image and locate the letters for the first-class lever. The *M* and *E* will be on top of the lever on the ends and the *F* will be under the lever, approximately in the middle.

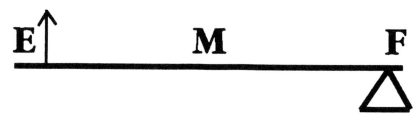

7. Then return to the second-class lever pattern with the *E* and *F* on either end and the *M* in the middle. All letters are now on top of the line.

8. You are now ready to begin the "second-class levers" activity.

---

second-class levers

MAIN IDEA: A second-class lever is one in which the mass is placed between the fulcrum and the force.

PROCESS SKILLS: Classifying
Interpreting data
Measuring
Predicting

MATERIALS:
Lever
Masking tape
Mass
Spring scale

TIME: 45 minutes

Again, this experiment works well if the students work in pairs.

PROCEDURE:
1. To prepare for this experiment, twist the clip on the lever so that it faces to the side with the numbers.

2. A large mass is fine for this experiment. Ask the students to weigh their masses and record the weight on the activity sheet.

3. Demonstrate how to set up the experiment.

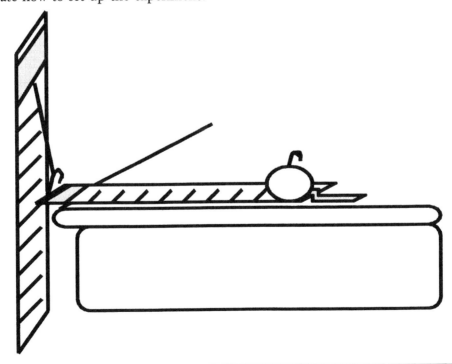

a. Place the lever so just the hook is exposed over the edge of the desk.

b. Take about 3 inches of masking tape and secure the lever to the desk. The point you tape to the desk is the fulcrum, or the point on which the lever pivots.

c. Take about 2 more inches of tape, curl it into a circle with the sticky side out, and place it on the lever at the 2-inch mark. This is a good time to review the concept of *fulcrum distance* (the distance between the fulcrum and the mass).

d. Attach the rubber band on the spring scale to the hook on the lever so that the force can be applied in an upward direction. It is important to note that the force is now being applied in the same direction as the mass is traveling.

4. When the students have set up the experiment to your satisfaction, direct their attention to the activity sheet. Before they make the first trial, ask them to make a prediction for the first trial only. They are recording how much force they think it will take to lift the mass using the lever. Before each successive trial, ask the students to make a prediction. Each time they should become more accurate.

5. Now the students should test the amount of force it will take them to lift the mass with fulcrum distances of 2 inches, 4 inches, 6 inches, 8 inches, 10 inches, and 12 inches, recording the amount of force for each distance on the activity sheet.

The second-class lever is very efficient in terms of mechanical advantage. Because the force always travels farther than the mass, it will always make things easier to lift. However, the disadvantage to the second-class lever is that when you have a lot of mechanical advantage you cannot lift the mass very far. Wheelbarrows and hand trucks use this principle for lifting while nutcrackers and wrenches utilize the principles for applying force.

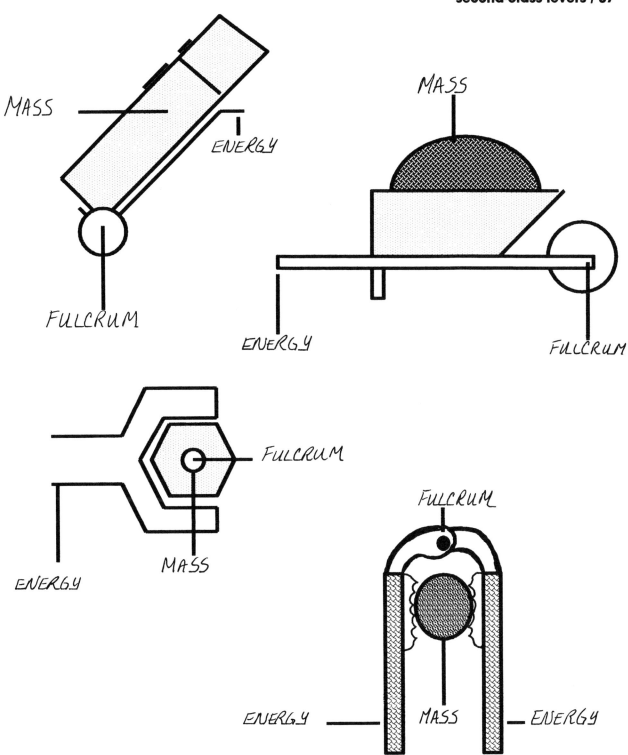

NAME_____

DATE_____

———————— **second-class levers** ————————

1. Use your spring scale to find the weight of your mass. Remember that to apply force you have to push up. Look at the end of the rubber band for your point of reference.

   My mass weighs _____ units.

2. Set up your experiment so that the fulcrum distance is 2 inches. Predict how much force it will take to lift your mass and write your prediction in the chart.

3. Try it out! How much force did it really take? Were you close? Record the information on the chart.

4. Now continue the pattern. Add 2 inches to the fulcrum distance, predict how much force it will take, and try it out and record the results.

Trial	Fulcrum distance	How much force do you think it will take?	Actual force
1			
2			
3			
4			
5			

5. Graph the results on the next page.

6. From the graph, see if you can figure out when there is mechanical advantage using the second-class lever. Tell why.

_____

_____

_____

_____

_____

_____

_____

_____

_____

_____

graphing the results

Lever class_____   Name_____

                                 Date_____

1. Transfer the data from your activity sheet to the table below
2. Draw a horizontal line at the weight of the mass
3. Locate your coordinates (points)
4. Connect the points with a "broken" line

Weight of the mass	units					
Fulcrum distance						
Force						

F
O
R
C
E

```
0"    2"    4"    6"    8"    10"    12"
FULCRUM DISTANCE
```

INTERPRETING THE GRAPHS

The graphed results for the second-class lever appear to be quite different than the results for the first-class lever. After drawing the line for the weight of the mass and then plotting the points, you will notice that the graph lies completely below the dark line. There is nothing wrong! Remember that a simple machine helps us do work by trading force for distance. No matter the location of the mass, the force always travels farther than the mass. Again, the proximity to the fulcrum is important. The closer to the fulcrum, the less force it takes to do the job. The disadvantage to this lever system occurs when you want to accomplish two functions: reducing the force and moving the mass a greater distance.

The value of this class of lever is that it is the easiest to use to apply a lot of force to the mass because the force and the mass are traveling in the same direction. With the hand truck all you want to do is lift the refrigerator a short distance from the floor before you roll it away. The same is true with the wheelbarrow. Think about using a wrench with a sticky bolt or nut. A lot of force needs to be applied to break the two loose. It is most useful if the force travels in the same way that you want the nut to turn. It is hard enough to keep track of which way to turn the wrench without having to think about turning the wrench in the opposite direction.

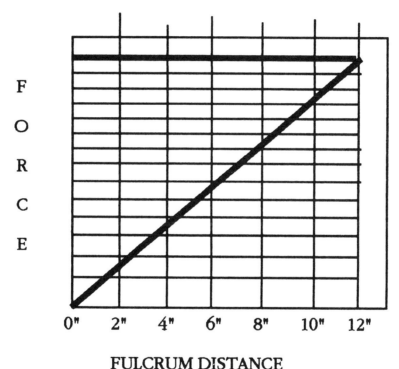

FULCRUM DISTANCE

more dots

MAIN IDEA: A third-class lever has the energy (force) located between the mass and the fulcrum.

PROCESS SKILLS: Inferring
Predicting

MATERIALS:
1 cutout of the letters *E*, *F*, and *M*
Overhead projector

TIME: 10 minutes

This is a good anticipatory set for the "third-class levers" activity to follow. The letters stand for:

E = Energy/force (to avoid confusion with the fulcrum)
F = Fulcrum
M = Mass

PROCEDURE:
1. The students should recognize these letters from the set for the "second-class levers" activity. Review the combinations for the parts of the lever systems for the first- and second-class levers. Use the shadow of a pencil or pen to represent the position of the lever. Locate the letters around the lever.

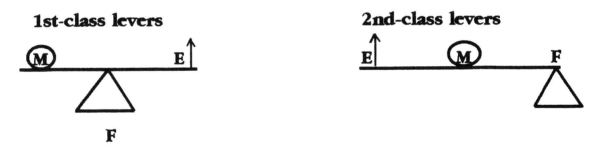

2. Next, challenge the students to write down a new combination of letters that they haven't had before. Remind them that by reversing the ends they have not really made a new combination, just changed the orientation in space.

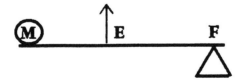

---

3. Quickly go around the room and monitor to find out who has been able to make the new combination. This is easy for you because all you have to look for is the *E* in the middle of the combinations.

first-class	MFE
second-class	EMF
third-class	MEF

4. Write the 3 patterns on the overhead to review the lever classes.

5. You should now be ready to head off on the "third-class levers" activity.

third-class levers

MAIN IDEA: The force is applied between the fulcrum and the mass in the third-class lever.

The third-class lever is useful for reaching.

It always sacrifices force for distance.

PROCESS SKILLS: Interpreting data
Measuring
Predicting

MATERIALS:
Lever
Masking tape
Mass
Jumbo paper clips
Spring scale

TIME: 45 minutes

This is an activity where the students should work as pairs for the purpose of materials manipulation.

PROCEDURE:
1. Before you start the actual experimentation you will need to make some modifications to the lever.

    a. First, rotate the hook so it faces down and away from the numbers.

    b. Then make a decision about which way will work best for you because there are two ways to approach the fulcrum distance measurement. If you want the numbering scheme to go from smaller to larger (natural order), remove the tape holding the hook and move it to the other end of the lever and tape it in place. OR, you can keep the assembly the same and work backward from the 12, which means that you will have to demonstrate to the class that 12 inches - 10 inches = 2 inches.

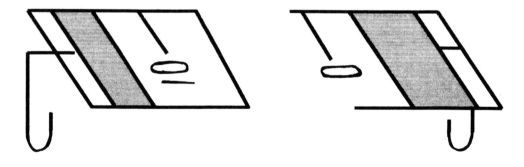

c. In either case you will need to make an attachment to the lever. Bend a jumbo paper clip open to about a 75-degree angle. Slide the larger loop over the lever, allowing you to apply force to the lever.

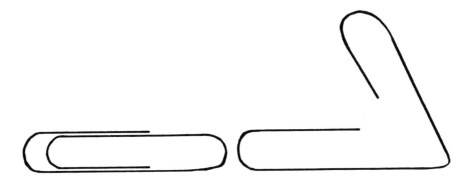

2. Now you are ready to set up the lever system with the students. Here are a couple of hints that could help you out:

a. Use the smallest masses possible as you will soon tax the ability of the spring scale as the force moves away from the mass.

b. Caution the students about trying to apply the force too close to the fulcrum. There is a tendency for that end of the lever to try and flip up.

3. Place the lever parallel and adjacent to the edge of a table or desk with the hook just over the edge of the desk.

4. Slide the paper clip loop over the lever with the vertical loop next to the edge of the desk.

5. Take about 4 inches of tape and attach the "0" end of the lever to the desk; this is the fulcrum or point on which the lever pivots.

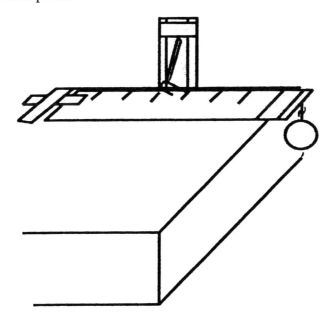

6. Have the students find the weight of their mass and record it on their activity sheet.

7. Ask them to predict how much force they think it will take to lift the mass with the force located 2 inches from the mass, and record the prediction on the activity sheet.

8. The students should now attach the mass to the hook of the lever hanging out over the edge of the table.

9. Hook the spring scale to the slide clip and apply the force to the lever through the slide.

10. The students should record the results and predictions for 2 inches, 4 inches, 6 inches, and 8 inches. Depending on the strength of the spring scale or weight of the mass, they probably won't be able to go any farther. The third-class lever gives us the ability to reach, at the expense of force. A good example of this is a crane. The crane is primarily used to lift things or reach things out and over open spaces. If you look closely at the arm of the crane, you will notice that the block and tackle or hydraulic ram is located partway out the boom, but the lift of the crane always takes place at the end of the boom. Therefore, it requires greater force to lift the object than its weight because the weight is traveling farther than the force being exerted.

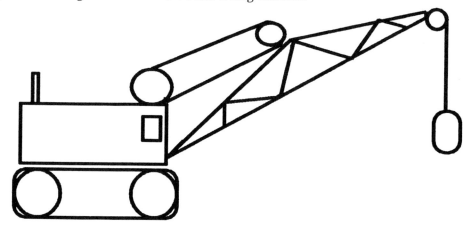

You might ask the students why we have fishing poles. The obvious "to catch fish" is the usual reaction. But upon probing, they should be able to determine that one of the reasons is to reach the bait out into deeper water, or to more desirable haunts. Or, perhaps, the real reason is to make the fish feel bigger—with a long pole, the fish is exerting much more leverage and therefore feels much heavier!

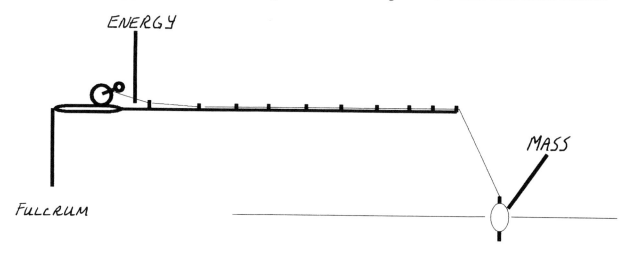

See if the students can come up with other real-life examples of third-class levers. It is hoped that one example that will come to mind will be their arms. If not, reach out and pick up something.

Talk about the attachment of the muscle to the ulna and radius. The muscle must be terribly strong to do the lifting. If the bicep were attached closer to the wrist, the muscle would be much less strong ... but contemplate what our shirtsleeves would look like!

NAME_____

DATE_____

———————— third-class levers ————————

1. Use your spring scale to find the weight of your mass. Remember that to apply force you have to push up. Look at the end of the rubber band for your point of reference.

    My mass weighs _____ units.

2. Set up your experiment so that the fulcrum distance is 2 inches. Predict how much force it will take to lift your mass and write your prediction in the chart.

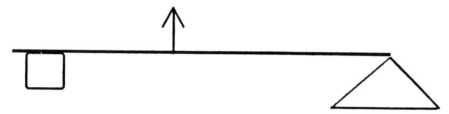

3. Try it out! How much force did it really take? Were you close? Record the information on the chart.

4. Now continue the pattern. Add 2 inches to the fulcrum distance, predict how much force it will take, and try it out. Record the results.

Trial	Fulcrum distance	How much force do you think it will take?	Actual force
1			
2			
3			
4			
5			

5. Graph the results on the next page.

6. From the graph, see if you can figure out when there is a mechanical advantage to using the third-class lever. Tell why.

_____

_____

_____

_____

_____

_____

_____

_____

_____

_____

_____

graphing the results

Lever class_____

Name_____

Date_____

1. Transfer the data from your activity sheet to the table below
2. Draw a horizontal line at the weight of the mass
3. Locate your coordinates (points)
4. Connect the points with a "broken" line

Weight of the mass		units					
Fulcrum distance							
Force							

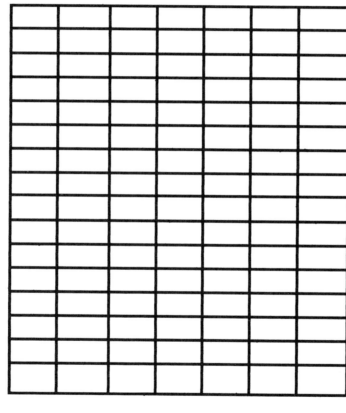

F
O
R
C
E

0"   2"   4"   6"   8"   10"   12"
FULCRUM DISTANCE

INTERPRETING THE GRAPHS

Congratulations for making it through the most perplexing of the lever systems or, for that matter, any of the simple machines activities. The difficulty with this system arises because there is always a sacrifice of force for distance. Whenever you locate the force between the fulcrum and the mass, the mass will always travel the longest distance. In this instance you have traded distance for force, or the inverse of why simple machines help us do work.

When you look at the graph, you see that a dramatic change in result has occurred. Before the pictorial representation was made you probably expected this because large amounts of force were required to complete the trials, and, in fact, you probably were not able to extend the fulcrum distance beyond 6 or 8 inches. The graph always lies above the heavy line depicting the weight of the mass.

The generalization this time is that the farther the force is away from the fulcrum, the easier it is to lift the mass. You will find this to be true when you inspect the construction of most machinery that applies to third-class levers. The machines are built for power. A simple demonstration with the students is to ask them to hold a book in each hand, with one close to the body and the other at arm's length. Which one fatigues the quickest? Remember, the human arm is a third-class lever.

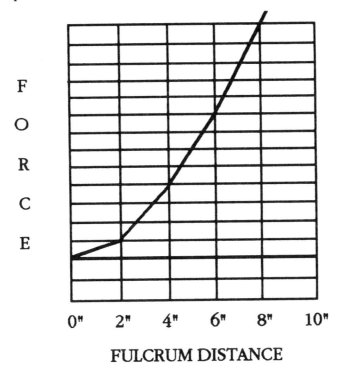

F
O
R
C
E

0"   2"   4"   6"   8"   10"

FULCRUM DISTANCE

To catch bigger fish, always use a longer pole!

---

cantilevers

MAIN IDEA: A cantilever is a lever with one end supported and the other end free.

A cantilever is commonly used in construction for decks, balconies, or the benches on a picnic table.

PROCESS SKILLS: Interpreting data
Measuring
Predicting

MATERIALS:
Levers
Rulers
Standardized masses (pennies, washers, paper clips, tacks, etc.)

TIME: 45 minutes

This is a good activity to work in pairs or groups.

PROCEDURE:
1. Show a picture of a cantilevered deck, balcony, picnic table, or bench. Ask the students how weight can be added to the platform if it is not supported somehow. The bench of a picnic table is attached to the table, but not supported from below so the real question is, How many people could you put on one bench before the table tips over?

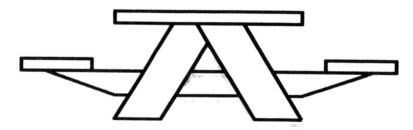

2. Lay the lever perpendicular to and across the edge of a table so it is just in balance.

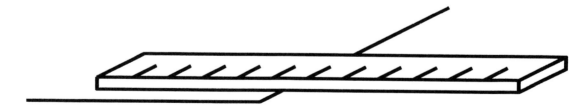

3. Direct the students to place 4 units in a pile 3 inches from the edge of the table on the table side.

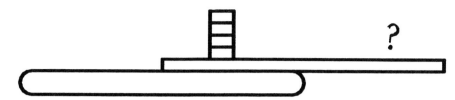

4. Ask the students to predict how many units it will take to tip the lever if they pile the units 2 inches out from the edge of the table.

5. Share the predictions and ask for supporting reasons.

6. Refer to the mass piled over the table as the counterbalance. The unsupported part of the lever is the load arm. The students should be directed to experiment with varying amounts of mass for the counterbalance at varying distances from the fulcrum (edge of the table), compared to how much mass is required on the load arm at varying distances in order to tip the cantilever.

7. Refer the students to the activity sheet titled "cantilevers." Demonstrate how they should record the predictions, weights, and distances. When they have recorded each trial they should find the mathematical product relationship for the counterbalance and the load arm and compare the products. In the demonstrated example above we would find:

    weight of counterbalance x distance to fulcrum = 4 x 3 = 12
    weight of load x distance to the fulcrum   = 6 x 2 = 12

    As they see the pattern developing their predictions should become very precise.

8. Now we are ready to get tricky! The students should make multiple piles of weights at several distances from the fulcrum for the counterbalance, for example, 2 units at 2 inches, 4 units at 4 inches, and 2 units at 6 inches. Then they should try to match the complex counterbalance either with a single pile at a single distance [(2 x 2) + (4 x 4) + (6 x 2)] = 32 units or 8 units at 4 inches (8 x 4) = 32; or multiple piles at multiple distances: 2 units at 2 inches and 7 units at 4 inches [(2 x 2) + (7 x 4) = 32].

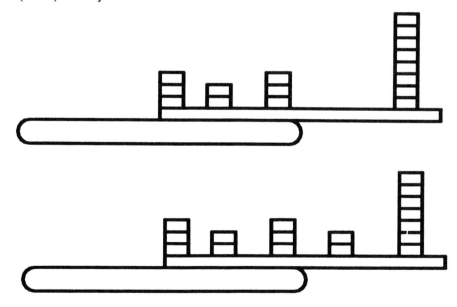

—— cantilevers ——

Name _____

Date _____

Fill in the table as you experiment with cantilevers. Record the number of units in a pile and the distance the pile is from the fulcrum (edge of the table). If you have more than one pile of units during a trial, list all of the piles separately in the same box.

Trial #	Number of units	Distance from fulcrum	# Units x Distance	How many units will it take?	If the load is ___ inches from the fulcrum	How many did it take?	# Units x Distance

What conclusions can you make about the loads and distances on both sides of the fulcrum?

_____

_____

_____

_____

deflection

MAIN IDEA: The load applied to a lever can affect its performance and must be considered in its construction.

PROCESS SKILLS: Inferring
Interpreting data
Measuring
Observing

MATERIALS:
Activity sheets titled "deflection"
Masking tape
Notebook paper
Paper clips
Standard masses
Wire hangers

TIME: 30 minutes

PROCEDURE:

1. Cut the base from a wire hanger, leaving a hook on one end.

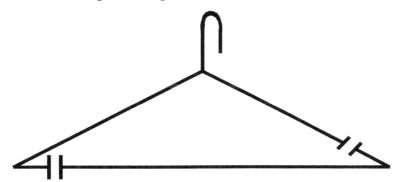

2. Locate a desk or table close to a wall.

3. Place the wire on the table parallel to and as near the wall as possible. Expose as much wire as you can beyond the edge of the table and secure the anchor end on the table with masking tape and a heavy object.

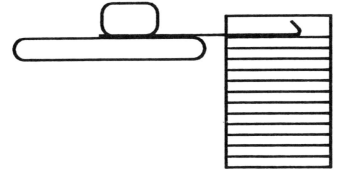

4. Number the lines of the notebook paper sequentially down along the margin line with line zero (0) being the top line of the paper.

5. Tape the paper to the wall so that the margin line is perpendicular to the floor and the zero line matches the wire.

6. Make a C-shaped hook by opening a paper clip and suspend it from the hook at the end of the lever (wire).

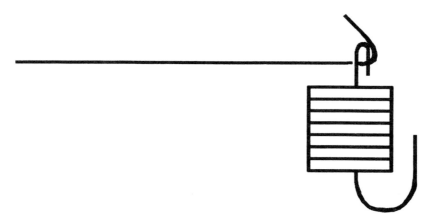

7. Explain that to perform the experiment, the students will be adding standard weights to the paper clip hook and recording how much the lever will deflect (bend) as a result of the addition of each weight. Before each weight is added, the students should record a prediction of how far they think the lever will deflect as a result of the additional weight.

8. As an extension of the information collected, the students should graph the results of the experimentation.

9. If you wish to extend the experimentation component, you could:

   a. vary the length of the load arm exposed beyond the edge of the table, or

   b. find hangers of different thicknesses, or

   c. use rulers instead of wire, or

   d. select materials other than wire.

   Discussion of the results of the experimentation is important. You could begin by brainstorming examples where this occurs in natural or built (human-made) environments. Nature and humans employ similar engineering principles to compensate for the phenomenon of deflection. Examples in nature would be the branches of a tree, the shaft of a feather, and our own arms and legs. The lever tapers more dramatically as it gets farther away from the point of attachment and gets closer to the load. If you experimented to find out what happens if you shortened the length of the load arm, your results should show there is less deflection as the length of the load arm shortens. When we build things where the load is applied to the end of an exposed lever (cantilevered), material and cost savings can be made by tapering the lever as it gets closer to the load. Examples of this kind of construction are diving boards, the arms that extend stoplights out over traffic lanes for greater visibility, and fishing poles.

---

deflection

Name_____

Date_____

What kind of standard units did you use?_____
Before you add units to the hook, predict how far you think the lever will bend. Record your prediction in the table. Then add the weight to the hook. Observe and record your result in the table below.

Number of units	How far do you think the lever will deflect?	How far did the lever deflect?

graphing deflection

Name_____

Date_____

Now that you have experimented with the amount a lever deflects or bends, it is time to graph the results. Notice that the units have not been included on the grid. Divide your total number of units by 20 and label the lines.

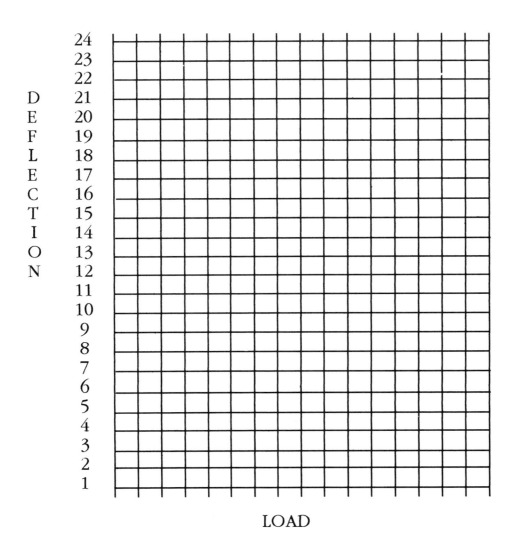

LOAD

catapults

MAIN IDEA: A catapult is an example of a third-class lever because the force is applied between the fulcrum and the mass.

PROCESS SKILLS: Measuring
Observing
Predicting

MATERIALS:
Rubber bands
Tinker toys or similar building kits

TIME: 30 minutes (plus time for extension and invention)

You will be building a prototype for a catapult. The students should be encouraged to go on and build their own out of materials that can be acquired from around the house.

PROCEDURE:
1. For the frame of the catapult you will need 6 wheel sprockets and 6 straight pieces. The straight pieces should be in sets of 2 and should be approximately on the proportions of 3, 4, 5, or the sides of a right triangle.

2. Build 2 identical (congruent) right triangles.

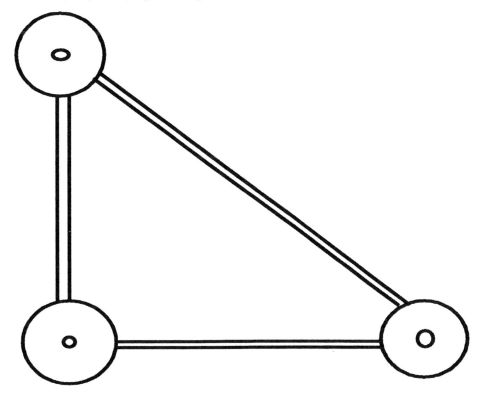

3. You will need 1 straight piece, 1 plastic spindle, and 1 wheel sprocket for the catapult arm. The straight piece should be longer than the height of the triangle. Attach the spindle to one end of the straight piece and the wheel sprocket to the other end so that the hole in the spindle is parallel to the flat side of the wheel sprocket.

4. Now select 3 straight pieces that are the same length. These straight pieces will finish the frame of the catapult.

5. Lay one of the triangles flat on the table in front of you. Insert the 3 straight frame pieces.

6. Slide the plastic spindle over the frame piece that is the vertex of the right angle so the arm extends out over the hypotenuse (longest side). Loop the rubber band loosely over the frame piece above the spindle. This is the apex of the triangle. If you haven't noticed, this is a perfect time to integrate mathematics into your science with the study of right triangles!

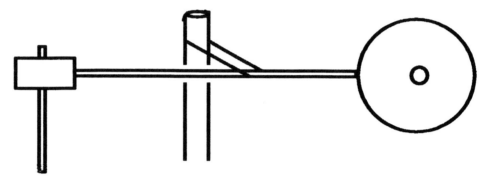

7. Place the second triangle above the first and press it onto the 3 frame pieces.

8. Set the catapult in an upright position and stretch the rubber band over the catapult frame.

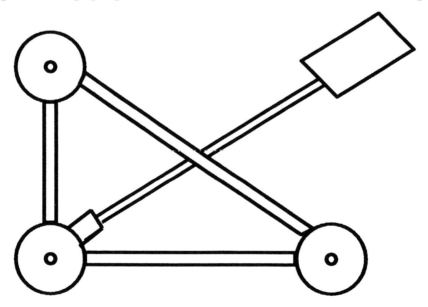

9. Let the experimentation begin! There are any number of variables that you can test for, such as:

    a. how far will the projectile travel;

    b. how close to a target can you land the projectile;

    c. how consistently can you land a projectile in a given spot;

    d. what happens if you change the length of the catapult arm;

    e. what happens if you change rubber bands;

    f. how can you modify the frame to change the flight path of the projectile;

    g. what is the best shape of projectile; or

    h. how does the weight of the projectile relate to the flight path?

Obviously, the experimentation can be extended quite far. Now that the students have the prototype of the catapult, challenge them to extend the construction on their own. The project also interfaces quite nicely with the study of medieval times.

draw me

Name_____

Date_____

Draw several different kinds of levers in action.

3
THINGS THAT TURN

Rollin', rollin', rollin', keep those ... sorry, some of you are probably too young to remember the TV show "Rawhide." Actually, *I'm* almost too young to remember it. In this section we will be looking at a series of activities that relate to the wheel and axle.

The wheel and axle is a simple machine made up of two parts, the wheel and the axle. All this means is that there is something round that turns around a rod. For my thinking, it has always been easiest to lump all of the variations of this pattern into one group. The variations are the pulley, which is a wheel that turns on an axle and has a groove around the outside edge, and the gear, which is a wheel that turns on an axle and has teeth around the outside edge. In any case, the basic shape is the same, and it helps us do work by trading force for distance. You might find these variations treated separately in other resources, but I believe there is no need to make something complicated that isn't.

There is just one little thing about how the wheel and axle work together. In both cases, the machine is the same. Case 1 is where the wheel turns independent of the axle. This would be like the front wheel of a bicycle, the wheels of a skateboard, or the wheel on a wheelbarrow. In all of these examples it is more important that the force be distributed over a longer distance to reduce friction, rather than they have the ability to apply force through the wheel and axle as a driving force. Examples of this second case would be the back wheel of your bicycle, the handle of a pencil sharpener, a screwdriver, or a doorknob.

Let's take a minute and consider the doorknob. I am intimately aware of doorknobs at the moment as we are adding on to our house and I am up to my elbows in the construction. Humor me and pretend that this is a round doorknob that is being installed. When you get ready to open a conventional door with a conventional knob, you grasp the round doorknob. Somehow force is transferred from your hand through the knob, and the door latch releases. This means that everything is somehow connected in there and that nothing is freewheeling or gliding. Therefore, the knob is directly attached to the shaft, which is actually square (case 2 of the wheel and axle, right?). Because the force you apply to the outside of the knob is traveling a much greater distance than the shaft, it is helping you do work. When the square shaft turns, it pulls the latch back toward the door, and the latch releases. Imagine what it would be like if you were trying to grasp that little shaft, about the size of a pencil, with your hand to release the latch.

Staying with our analogy of the doorknob for just a minute longer, let's consider another set of the wheel and axle—hinges. These are not what we normally think of as a wheel and axle, but they definitely fit the definition. The wheel is the frame that is attached to the door and the jamb, and the axle is the pin that holds the two frames together. The two frames move independently of the pin and rotate around it.

Another fixed axle combination is a screwdriver. The round or nearly round handle is larger than the metal tip, which is inserted into the screw head. Your hand, which is applying the force, travels a much greater distance than the head of the screw, so a greater amount of force is being applied to the screw, making it easier to insert or extract it from the metal or wood.

Gears are toothed wheels. The teeth of one gear fit into the grooves between the teeth of another gear. Sometimes the gears turn independently on axles, in which case the force is only being made to reverse direction. In other circumstances, the gears are fixed to the axle, and force is transferred to a useful purpose through another gear or sometimes a chain. Mechanical advantage occurs when the two gears are not the same size. If a little gear is turning a big gear, the big one will turn much slower as the small gear will go around several times before the big one will (this must be trading force for distance!). The reverse is also true. If the big gear is turning the little one, each time the big one turns the little one will go around several times, requiring more force. You have experienced this when you rode a bicycle with multiple gears. If the sprocket in the front is a lot bigger than the one in the back, it is much harder to pedal but useful when you go downhill and want to turn the back wheel faster. The process is reversed when you want to go uphill.

If you want to find out how much the difference is, there is an easy arithmetic problem you can use. Just count the number of teeth around the outside edge of each gear. Then divide the small number into the bigger one. This will tell you how many times the small gear turns for each single revolution of the large gear.

The wheel and axle is relatively simple. A wheel, something round, turns around or with the axle. If the wheel is smooth, it is a wheel. If it has a groove in which you can place some kind of rope, it is a pulley. And, if there are teeth along the outside edge, then it is a gear. In all of the situations, they are basically the same.

toy trucks

MAIN IDEA: The wheel and axle is a simple machine.

The wheel and axle helps us do work by trading force for distance.

PROCESS SKILLS: Interpreting data
Measuring

MATERIALS:
Masses
Spring scales
Toy cars or trucks

TIME: 30 minutes

Have the students work in pairs.

PROCEDURE:
1. Several days before conducting the activity, ask the students to bring toy cars or trucks from home. As the students get older, you might suggest that because you know that they are much too mature to still have such things around, a younger brother or sister might have one that could be borrowed for a day or so for science.

2. Open a paper clip to a C shape and attach it to the front of the vehicle. To the C-clip you will attach the spring scale so that the vehicle can be pushed along the floor.

3. Refer the students to the data sheets. Have them find the weight of their masses and record the results on the data sheets. Ask them to measure the height of the wheels on the vehicle and record it on the sheet.

4. Ask the students to record how much force they think it will take them to move the truck along the floor.

5. Place the mass in the vehicle, attach the spring scale to the front of the vehicle, and push it along the floor. The students should record the "average" amount of force required to move the vehicle while applying steady pressure.

6. When the students have recorded the results using their own vehicle, ask them to trade and repeat the experiment several times.

7. When they have collected a significant amount of data, ask them to see if they can determine if there is a relationship between the height of the wheel and the amount of force it takes to move the mass.

8. Other variables that you might want to consider are number of wheels or widths of wheels.

9. Follow up with a discussion of the results. You might notice that there is a relationship between wheel height and the amount of force it takes to move the mass. However, there are quite a number of factors to consider when you discuss this activity. First, the weight of the mass will not have much to do with how much force it takes to move the truck as all of the weight is now being borne by the wheels and you are really only measuring the amount of friction between the wheels and the floor and axles. The friction is now reduced to the number of points of contact and the amount of contact of the wheel on the floor. If the truck has four wheels, then the weight is divided by four, and so on for the number of wheels. Now, as the height of the wheel grows, the proportional amount of contact surface is reduced, and the wheel should roll much more easily.

toy trucks

Name _____

Date _____

Vehicle number	Weight of mass	Number of wheels	How much force will it take to move?	Actual force to move the truck.

Explain why the amount of force was so much different from the weight of the mass. _____

Does the difference in the height of the tires seem to make any difference? Why? Why not? _____

Describe the truck that was easiest to move. Try to tell what helped make this the best for the job. _____
_____
_____

windlass

MAIN IDEA: The windlass is a wheel and axle that lifts or hoists.

The wheel and axle helps us do work by trading force for distance.

PROCESS SKILLS: Inferring
Interpreting data
Measuring

MATERIALS:
Flex straws
Masking tape
Masses
Paper clips
Portion cups
Sand or pebbles
String (24 inches per group)

TIME: 45 minutes

This is a good activity for students to work in groups of two.

PROCEDURE:
1. Each group will need 3 paper clips, 2 flex straws, a piece of string, about 1 foot of masking tape, a portion cup, and some sand or pebbles for weight.

2. In the center of the long section of one flex straw, snugly tie one end of the string. Open a paper clip to the C shape and tie it to the other end of the string.

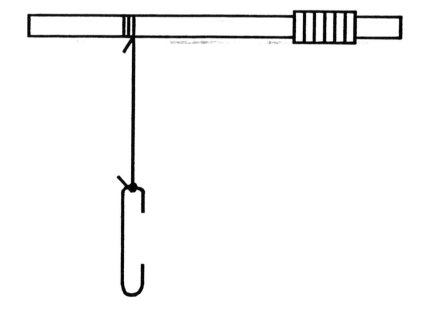

---

3. Open the two remaining paper clips to the C shape and then twist them so that one loop is at a right angle or 90 degrees to the other.

4. Tape one at the corner of a desk or table and the other parallel to the first and about 2 inches apart.

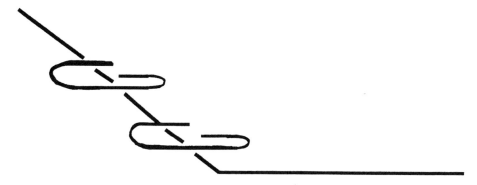

5. Slide the long section of the straw into the two loops so that the string is between the loops and hangs down toward the floor. Attach the portion cup to the paper clip hook close to the floor.

6. Fill the cup with sand or pebbles for weight.

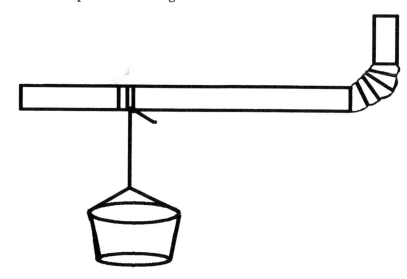

7. Pinch the long end of the second straw and insert it into the short end of the first straw. The windlass, or crank, is now constructed (see page 70).

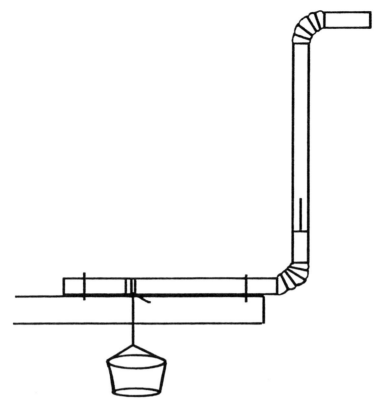

8.   The students now take turns cranking up the weight in the cup. Actual measurement of the force is difficult, but they can get a good sense of the comparative difference by feel. By placing the tip of the index finger on the vertical crank and turning, they can feel how much force it takes to lift the cup. After several rotations, they should slide their finger a little farther from the axle.

9.   Ask for comparisons and conclusions.

10.   By multiplying the distance their fingers are from the axle by 6 (an approximation of 2 x pi x radius) they can draw some mathematical comparisons of how much easier it is to lift the weight. These results could be graphed quite easily.

---

taming the lions

MAIN IDEA: The wheel and axle is a simple machine.

The block and tackle is a complex machine made up of fixed and movable pulleys.

PROCESS SKILL: Inferring

MATERIALS:
2 dowels or broom handles
20-30 feet of light rope or clothesline

TIME: 10 minutes for the first trial

This is a great activity for an anticipatory set for pulley and block and tackle activities.

PROCEDURE:
1. You will need 5 volunteers for this activity, 4 of substantial stature and 1 of much finer frame. (This is a setup!)

2. Tie a loop in one end of the rope. Feed the loop over the end of one of the dowels.

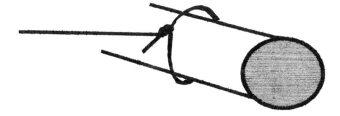

3. The 2 dowels will be parallel and about 2 feet apart. One larger volunteer should be on each end of a dowel, facing inward. They should stand with their arms extended fully.

4. Run the line around the dowels 3 or 4 times, feeding the loose end out and between one of the pairs of volunteers on the ends of one of the dowels.

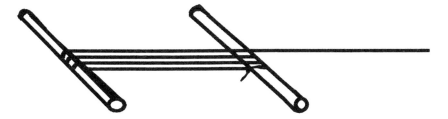

5. Have the slighter volunteer grasp the loose end of the line firmly and pull mightily. Probably, with much amazement, the burly beasts on the ends of the dowels will be drawn together.

Discussion of the results: This activity could be used as a set to pique the students' interest. A detailed explanation would work best after you have completed the following pulley and block and tackle activities.

There might need to be a little troubleshooting to fine-tune this activity. Because the size of the line and dowels does affect how easily the rope will slide over the dowels, there is a possibility that you could create too much friction by having too many wraps. Each time the line travels from one dowel to the next it reduces the amount of force necessary to complete the task. So if there are 3 loops, then there are 6 sections of line between the dowels, or the force has been multiplied by 6. The amount of force necessary to move a mass is equally divided between the number of strands that support the mass. A fourth loop would provide 8 strands, therefore magnifying the force 8 times!

fixed pulleys

MAIN IDEA: The fixed pulley is a simple machine.

The fixed pulley is a wheel and axle with a groove along the edge of the wheel to hold a line or rope.

The fixed pulley does not change the amount of force to perform a task, it only allows you to change the direction in which the force is applied.

PROCESS SKILLS: Interpreting data
Measuring

MATERIALS:
Masking tape
Masses
Paper clips
Pulleys
Spring scales
String

TIME: 45 minutes

Working in groups of two is *highly* recommended.

PROCEDURE:
1. Open a paper clip in a C shape. Tape it to the edge of a table or desk so that part of the large loop is exposed over the edge.

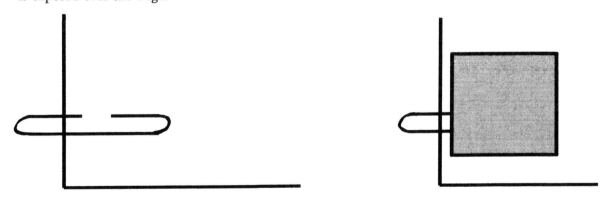

2. Attach the pulley to the wire loop hanging over the edge of the table (see page 74).

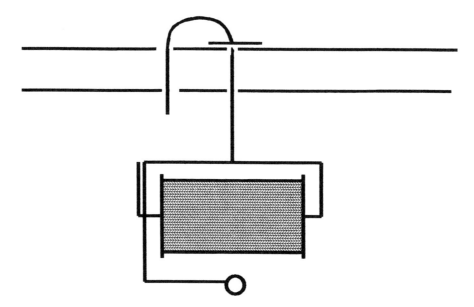

3. Each group will need about 3 feet of string. Have each partner hold one end of the string (extremely creative management technique!). Then double over about 3 inches of each end and tie a loop. This is done by wrapping the doubled end once around the end of the index finger, sliding the loop off the finger, and pulling the end through the loop. All this is is a simple overhand knot.

4. Feed one loop through the upper groove of the pulley.

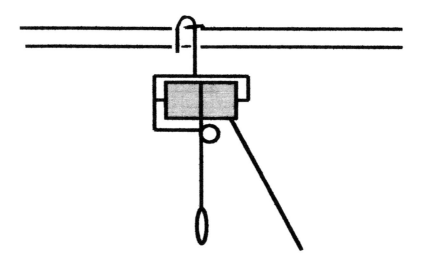

5. Attach the mass to one loop of the string (see page 75).

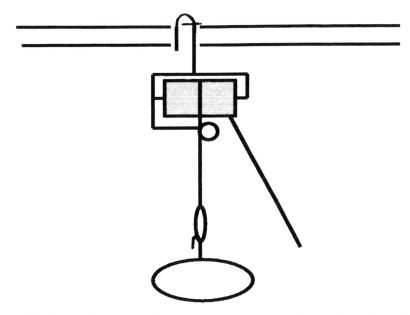

6. Open another paper clip into a C shape and use it to connect the spring scale to the other loop. Now you are ready to experiment!

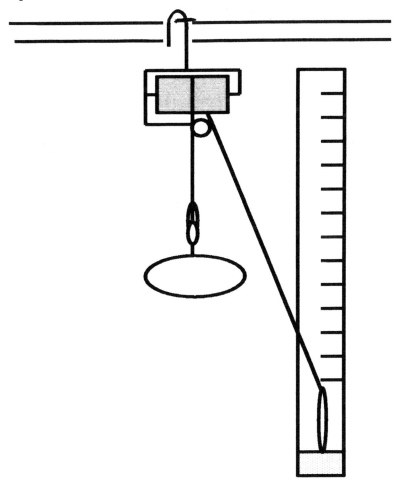

7. Refer the students to the activity sheet titled "fixed pulleys." Explain that they will be applying force to the mass through the spring scale. To predict how much force it will take to lift the mass, first have them find the weight of their mass and enter it on the activity sheet. Then demonstrate how they will be lifting the mass by applying force at various angles measured in relation to the string supporting the mass. These angles will be approximately 0 degrees, 22 degrees, 45 degrees, 67 degrees, and 90 degrees. Ask the students to write their first prediction on the sheet and then find out how much force it took to lift the mass. Then, have them make a prediction for the second trial before experimenting.

8. Complete the activity and sheets and then discuss the results.

Up to this point there has been a difference in the amount of force it has taken to complete the trials. Now there is little or no difference. This is due to the fact that the mass and the force are always traveling the same distance. If you wish to demonstrate this (which is always a good idea), make sure each group has two rulers. Have one partner measure how far the mass moves while the other measures how far the spring scale moves. Voilà! They are almost exactly the same for each trial. Simple machines only help us do work when they can trade force for distance.

When I was much younger, the neighbors had a hobby farm, and it was always great fun to go there during haying time. They had a barn with a hayloft, and I was always interested in the way they got the hay up into the loft. A single pulley was located on a track at the top of the door. A line went from the tractor through the pulley to the fork, which was rammed into the loose hay. Then the tractor would drive off, lift the hay up to the track, then run it into the barn and drop it in just the right spot. The point is that the tractor had more than enough force to lift the hay, but it could only travel along the ground, which was absolutely no good for lifting the hay up to the loft unless the direction of the force could be changed—thus the need for the fixed pulley.

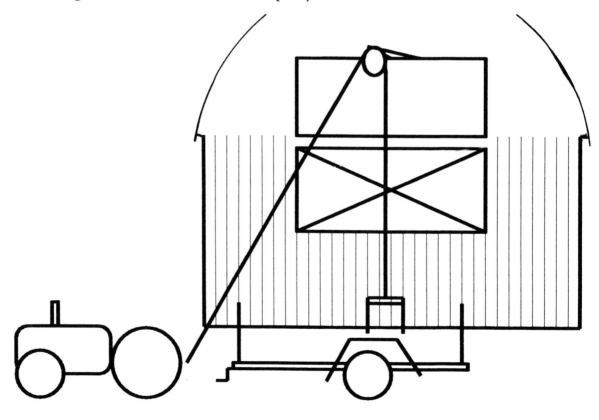

name
date

fixed pulleys

The weight of my mass is _____ units.

Trial #	Angle	How much force do you think it will take to lift the mass?	How much force did it take to lift the mass?

Why do you think the results came out the way they did? _____

movable pulleys

MAIN IDEA: The movable pulley is a simple machine.

The movable pulley is a wheel and axle with a groove along the edge of the wheel to hold a line or rope.

The movable pulley helps us do work by trading force for distance.

PROCESS SKILLS: Interpreting data
Measuring

MATERIALS:
Masking tape
Masses
Paper clips
Pulleys
Spring scales
String

TIME: 30 minutes

This is another activity that is *highly* recommended for groups of two.

PROCEDURE:
1. This activity assumes that you have already done the activity for "fixed pulleys." If not, then it will be very helpful for you to take a step back and review those directions, because there is only a slight modification in the setup to complete this activity.

2. Assume that you have the paper clip hook hanging over the edge of the desk or table, a pulley, a spring scale, a mass, and a string with a loop tied in each end.

3. Hook one loop of the string over the hook of the paper clip attached to the edge of the desk. Let the other end dangle freely.

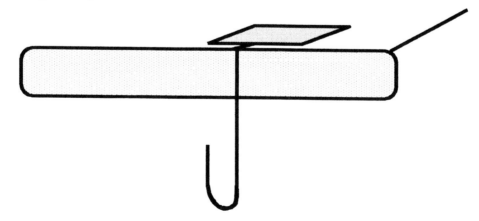

---

4. Attach the mass directly to the hook on the pulley and feed the loose end of the string through the groove of the pulley closest to the hook and mass.

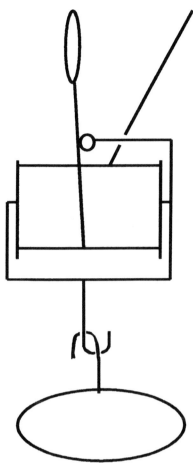

5. Attach the loose end of the string to the spring scale using one of those C-shaped paper clips. (By now you and the students should be really handy with applying force using the spring scale with a pushing rather than pulling motion!)

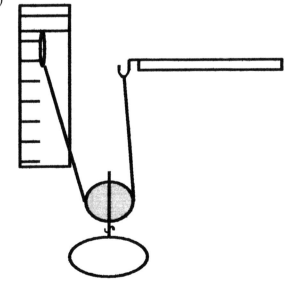

6. Repeat the trials using the angles that you used for the fixed pulley: 0 degrees, 22 degrees, 45 degrees, 67 degrees, and 90 degrees. The angle is still measured between the two strings. If you turned the last diagram upside down it would look almost identical to the fixed pulley. This effect could also be achieved by standing on your head, but it is much less practical.

7. Refer the students to the activity sheet titled "movable pulleys." Have them find and record the weight of their masses. Then, make predictions on how much force they think it will take to lift the mass. Complete the first trial and record the results on the sheet. Then the second prediction is made before the second trial is completed, and so on.

8. Complete the activity and discuss the results.

You will (should) find that the results are relatively consistent between the trials. As the angle gets a little closer to 90 degrees, the force might increase a little, but not significantly. It's one of those physics things relating to vectors. The results should show that the amount of force it takes to lift the mass is about one-half of the weight of the mass. To demonstrate the "why" of this is quite simple and should be done in two quick follow-up activities. The first is splitting the weight:

1. Feed the string through the pulley as if you were going to set up the movable pulley experiment. The variation is to hook a spring scale to each loop of the string. Notice that each spring scale is recording nearly one-half of the weight of the mass.

The second activity is measuring the motion:

1. Set up the movable pulley apparatus as if you were going to conduct the experiment. Each partner will need a ruler. Exert the force through the spring scale in a vertical direction. One partner should lift the spring scale exactly 1 foot. The other partner should measure how far the mass rises. They should find that the force travels twice as far as the mass. Simple machines help us do work by trading force for distance.

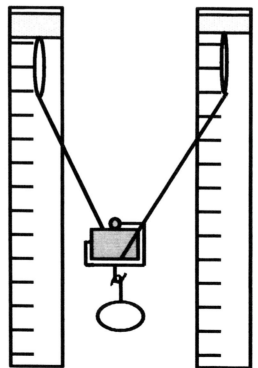

movable pulleys

name ——
date ——

The weight of my mass is _____ units.

Trial #	Angle	How much force do you think it will take to lift the mass?	How much force did it take to lift the mass?

Why do you think the results came out the way they did? ——

block and tackle

MAIN IDEA: The block and tackle is a compound machine made up of several simple machines.

The block and tackle is made up of fixed and movable pulleys.

The block is another name for the pulleys, and the tackle is another name for the lines or ropes.

The weight is evenly divided between the number of lines that support it.

PROCESS SKILLS: Inferring
Interpreting data
Measuring

MATERIALS:
Masking tape
Masses
Pulleys
Paper clips
Spring scales
String

TIME: 45 minutes

Working in pairs is a must in this activity.

PROCEDURE:
1. Tape a paper clip to the edge of the desk so that a loop extends out over the edge. Suspend a fixed pulley to the loop. Attach a mass to the hook of the movable pulley.

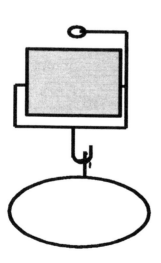
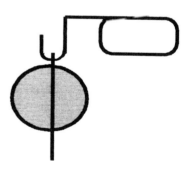

---

2. You will need about 4 feet of string for each of the groups. Again, tie a loop in each end of the string.

3. Feed one loop of the string through the top groove of the fixed pulley, down to the lower groove of the movable pulley, then back up to the hook that holds the fixed pulley. Attach it there.

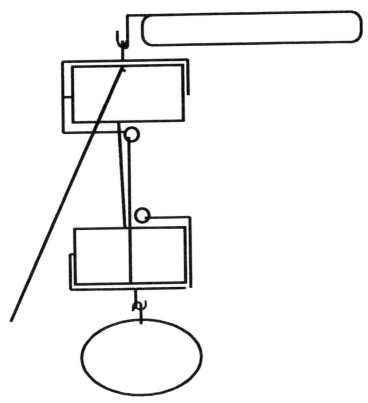

4. Attach the spring scale to the loose end of the string. Now force can be added to the string by pushing on the spring scale. The students should be able to find that the force can be added in just about any direction without any noticeable change in the amount of force that is needed to do the job (see page 84).

5. Discuss the results of their findings. You will notice that these findings are much the same as those of the movable pulley. See if the students can work out what the function of each of the pulleys is in the system. The top pulley, of course, is a fixed pulley and only changes direction and does not provide mechanical advantage. The lower pulley is a movable pulley and divides the force between two strings. When the string returns to the hook, the hook acts like an anchor. So, in reality, all this is is a complicated movable pulley.

6. Have the students extend one arm. Now have them rotate it in a clockwise fashion several times. They have now traced the path that they must keep in mind as they set up a more complex block and tackle system.

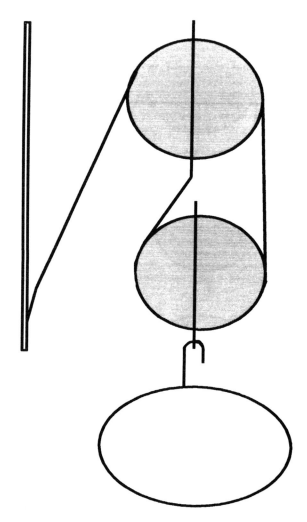

7. With one partner holding the movable pulley, the other should carefully detach the loop of the string attached to the desk. The loose end should be fed through the fixed (upper) pulley, then pulled down to the movable (bottom) pulley, through the pulley, and then back up to the hook and attached again (see page 85).

8. The students can now apply force through the spring scale. They should find a very significant difference in force that is needed to lift the mass. Ask the students to count the number of strings that are suspending the mass. If they divide the weight of the mass by 4, it should come out to be very close to the amount of force that was actually needed to lift the mass.

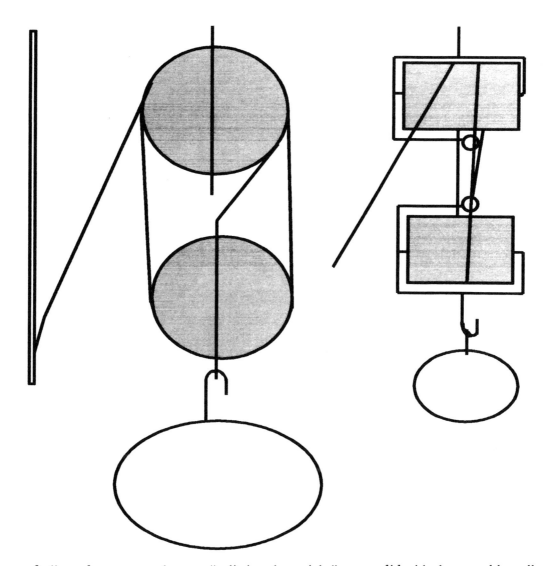

If you are feeling adventurous, then try "splitting the weight" as you did with the movable pulley. This time you will need two strings that are close to the same length with loops tied in the ends. In each loop place a C-shaped paper clip and attach it to a spring scale. The center of both loops should pick up the mass. You should find that the sum of the spring scales equals the weight of the mass (see top of page 86).

You can also "measure the distance." With the four-strand block and tackle in place, make measurements of how far the mass moves compared to how far the force has to move. You will find that the force has to travel four times as far as the mass (see bottom of page 86).

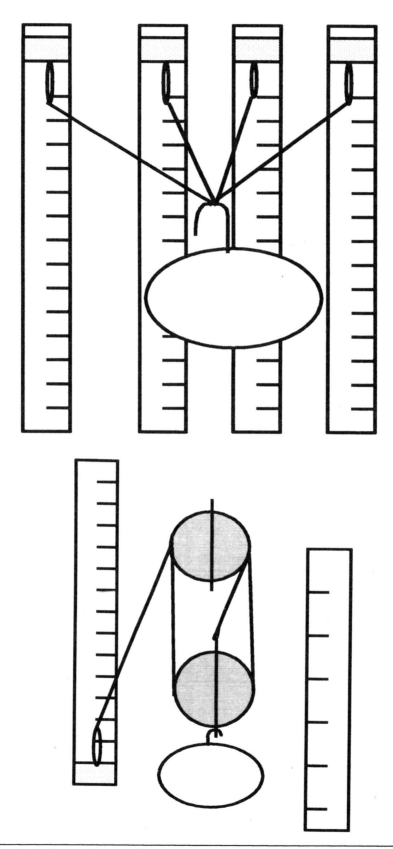

windmills

MAIN IDEA: A windmill is a form of a wheel and axle.

Energy from the wind can be used for the force needed to turn a wheel and axle.

PROCESS SKILLS: Inferring
Interpreting data
Measuring

MATERIALS:
3-by-5-inch pieces of railroad board or thin cardboard
Drinking straws cut to 6 inches
Hair dryer
Masking tape
Paper clips
Scissors
Shoe box
String
Wire hanger

TIME: 45 minutes for the prototype; 3 weeks for experimenting

PROCEDURE:
1. Hand out 2 pieces of railroad board, 6 inches of masking tape, 18 inches of string, a paper clip, and a straw to each student.

2. Have the students place the 2 cards on top of each other and trim them to the same size.

3. Have the students hold the 2 cards together in one hand by a corner so the cards are long from left to right.

4. Holding the scissors slightly open, slide them so they are ready to cut along the bottom edge so they end up at the middle of the cards.

5. Make a short cut up into the cards, set down the scissors, and open the cards as you would a book. The 2 short slits should match (see top of page 88).

6. Rotate 1 card a quarter turn and slide the 2 cards together. This will form the letter *X*, almost. This was a practice, as invariably if you ask the students to cut halfway across the cards, some will cut them in half (see page 88).

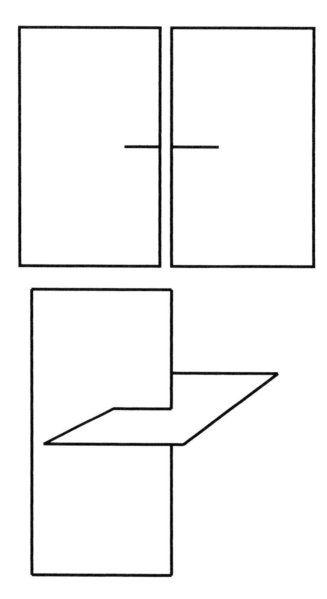

7. Slide the cards apart, rotate them so the slits match, and close them as you would a book. Cut the cards to nearly halfway and repeat the process of opening, turning, and sliding them together until the outside edges of the cards match. Lay the completed *X* on the table in front of you. These are the vanes of the windmill.

8. Lay the straw down into the top V of the vanes so that an equal amount extends past each side of the vanes. Take the 6 inches of tape and tear it into 4 equal pieces. Take 1 of the pieces of tape and secure the straw into the bottom of the V. Then attach a piece of tape on either side of the first. The frame of the windmill is now complete (see page 89).

(see page 89)

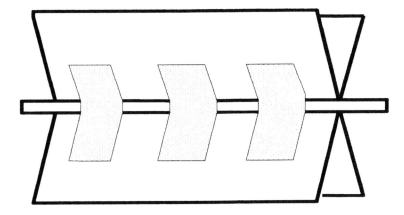

9. Turn the vanes on the table so that one end of the straw extends out over the edge of the desk. Take the string and drape about 4 inches (4 fingers) over the straw. Wrap the short end snugly (don't crush the straw) around the straw and tie it securely with a series of 2 or 3 knots.

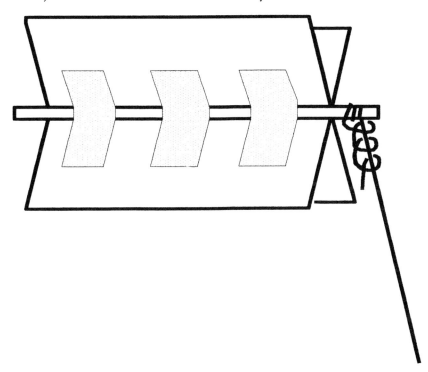

10. To the long end of the string tie a C-shaped paper clip. You will be attaching things to it that you want to lift later.

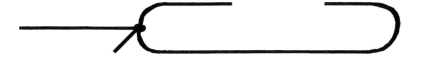

11. For your whole group, you will need a shoe box. Throw away the kid. Cut 2 small square notches out of the top long edges opposite each other. Directly under one of the notches on either side cut a 2-inch square hole in the bottom of the box.

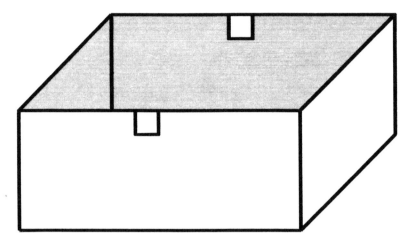

12. Cut the long straight wire from the bottom of a wire hanger. This will serve as a universal axle for all of the windmills. Just insert the wire into any of the straws, feed the paper clip and string down through the hole in the bottom of the box, attach a handy weight like a pen, pencil, or scissors, and turn on the wind!

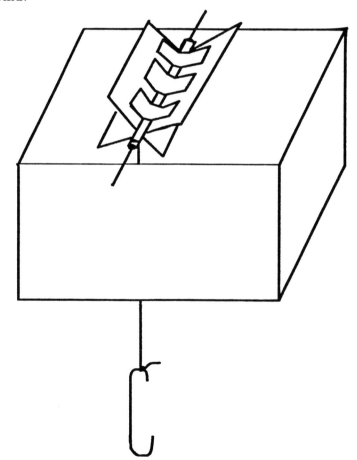

The challenge has only just begun! Now that the students know how to build the prototype, they can go on to build amazing contraptions using just the hair dryer for wind power. Three to 6 pounds is not an uncommon amount to be able to lift. Some time is usually spent on determining what variables can be changed, and how the machine can be made more efficient. It is also helpful for their planning if students are required to draw diagrams of what they will be attempting to build. You might also want to put some restrictions on size. Two students rose to the challenge. One was able to lift 69 pounds. (She was quite proud of herself!) Another student was up to 60 pounds when a small metal pulley split.

To demonstrate how the machine is helping to do work by trading force for distance, you can do a couple of things. First, have the students trace the path of the outside edge of one of the vanes with an index finger. Then have them trace the circumference of the straw. They should be able to see quite easily that the vane is traveling a much greater distance.

But, the visual is much more dramatic. Cut the string from the straw and tape it to the upper edge of one of the vanes. Then feed the string over the vanes and down through the hole. Blow against the vanes as you did before with the hair dryer. You will not be able to pick up a ballpoint pen with your prototype windmill.

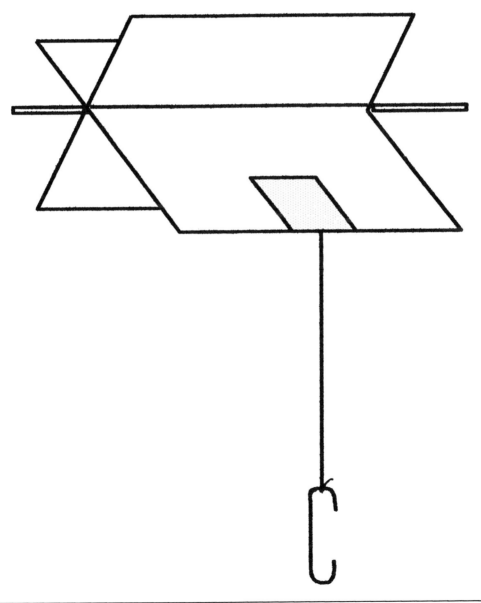

pulley geoboards

MAIN IDEA: A pulley is a simple machine.

The way in which a line crosses a pulley determines the way it turns.

The sizes of the connected pulleys determine the mechanical advantage.

PROCESS SKILLS: Interpreting data
Predicting

MATERIALS:
Hammer
Nails
Rubber bands
Scraps of wood
Empty thread spools

TIME: 30 minutes to build; variable times to experiment

Students can work alone or in small groups.

PROCEDURE:
1. Several weeks before conducting this activity, ask the students to collect as many empty thread spools as they can. It is also useful if you can bring in several old telephone books or thick catalogs. When you get ready to do the nailing, place the phone book on the desk, table, or floor and then put the wood on the book. This absorbs a lot of the shock, protects the surface from nails, and most important, keeps you friends with the rooms beside or below you!

2. When the students have amassed a collection of spools, have them place the spools randomly on the surface of the board.

3. Insert a nail in the hole in the spool and drive the nail into the board. The nail should not go completely through the board but should be in far enough so the spool turns freely and the nail and spool will not fall off of the board (see page 93).

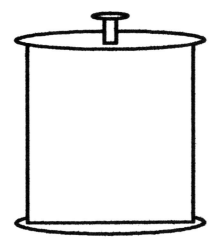

4. The boards are now ready to use. All you have to do is loop a rubber band over 2 or more pulleys, making sure that the rubber band is stretched slightly. It is helpful if you have a box of "assorted sizes" rubber bands handy. One partner should challenge the other to figure out which direction any pulley in a series will turn when another is rotated.

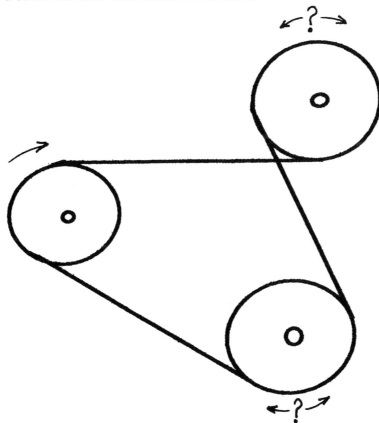

5. Make challenges for the students: The second pulley turns the same way as the first; the second pulley turns the opposite direction as the first; or, the second turns opposite the first while the third turns the same as the first. The combinations are many!

6. Now for the mechanical advantage part of this activity: Have the students place marks on the top surface of each spool that extend from the hole to the outer edge. The purpose of these marks is to establish a point of reference. Link any two pulleys together with a rubber band. Rotate the first pulley exactly one turn. The partner then counts the number of turns that the second pulley makes. The students should record their predictions and observations on the data sheet titled "geospools."

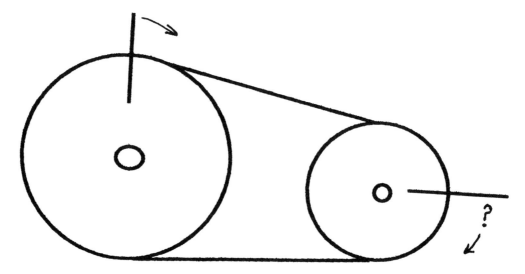

The circumference of the pulley determines the mechanical advantage when two or more pulleys are hooked in a series. If the pulleys are the same size, then there is no mechanical advantage because there is no trade of force for distance; both pulleys turn the same distance. When the drive pulley is larger, the second pulley will turn more turns. Because force is traded for distance, it will require more force to turn the drive wheel if there is a significant load applied. The opposite is true if the pulley sizes are reversed. If the drive pulley is smaller than the load pulley, it will take less force to turn the drive pulley because it will require more than one turn to rotate the load pulley if there is a significant load.

The best way to demonstrate this is to use a bicycle that has multiple gears. Turn the bicycle over so that it rests on the seat and handlebars. Compare the sizes of the sprockets in the front and the rear. Rotate the pedals and get a sense of how much force is required to turn the rear tire. Shift gears up and down and note where the most force is required and compare the sizes of the sprockets at different times. If you want, you could also measure the diameters of the gears at any particular time to calculate the mechanical advantage. Up until now the students have known how and when to change gears, but for most, there has never been any connection of what happens when they change gears. For once, science applies to their daily lives!

Speaking of oxymorons (jumbo shrimp), we have just made a very subtle paradigm shift that is important to note. When you turned the bicycle over, you were no longer experimenting with pulleys, but rather, gears. If you read the introduction to this section, you will remember that I lumped the wheel and axle, pulley, and gear all into one big happy family. This was done on purpose because they basically function in the same manner. The wheel/pulley/gear is round and is smooth/grooved/toothed on the outer edge. All rotate with or around an axle. So, to make simple machines as simple as possible, they are all grouped together. However, it is very important to note their similarities *and* differences.

GETTING IT IN GEAR

Here's a quick little variation on the same activity.

1. Raid a pop machine or have the students bring in a bunch of the twist-off type bottle caps ... probably most common on malt beverages. Nail them on a board in a line so that:

   a. they are bottom side up,

   b. they are interlocking, and

   c. they will turn.

This will give you a one-time demonstrator on gears. (Translation: Don't commit too much time to this one because its function is not very long lasting.)

The students should be able to notice that one gear turns the next, and that each successive gear turns in the opposite direction. This little bit of information alone will help them score at least 40 points higher on the Graduate Record Exams!

Remember in the good old days when watches were real and there were gears inside? All of those gears were important to make the hands turn at just exactly the right speed.

However, this demonstrator is a neat tool. Just throw on another row or two of bottle caps and you have a great fish scaler!

geospools

Name_____
Date_____

Label each of the spools on the board with a different letter. This will be important so that you can keep track of the spools with which you experiment. Then, draw a single line out from the center of each spool to the outside edge. This will help you keep track of how many times a spool turns. In this activity you will connect any two spools with a rubber band. Then you will turn either of the two spools. It will be your job to first, predict how many times spool #2 turns when you turn spool #1 exactly one turn. Second, you will count and record how many times spool #2 turns when you turn spool #1 exactly one turn.

Letter of spool #1	Letter of spool #2	How many times do you think spool #2 will turn when you turn spool #1 exactly one turn?	How many times did spool #2 turn when you turned spool #1 exactly one turn?

Do you think that there is a way to figure out how many times the second spool will turn mathematically? Try it!

mousetrap cars

MAIN IDEA: Building a mousetrap car is an excellent opportunity for a "product-post unit" evaluation. The student would be able to apply everything he or she has learned about the wheel and axle as well as the lever!

PROCESS SKILLS: Inferring
Interpreting data
Measuring
Predicting

MATERIALS:
The materials for this activity are best left to the creativity of the students as determined by their design for their cars.

TIME: Variable time in class and at home, determined by the involvement of the students. I would recommend that a 2-week time limit be set and that you have a "Derby Day" at the conclusion when all of the students can show off their vehicles.

PROCEDURE:
1. Tell the students that they are being asked to design a car using a mousetrap as the source of power. They must figure out how to get the energy out of the spring to drive the wheels. A review of fixed axles and free axles would be worthwhile. You can establish as many rules as you wish, however, the more constraints you place, the more you limit creativity.

2. Pass out the "Mousetrap Car Design Sheet" to the students. It will be useful for them to make a diagram of what they think their car might look like and how they plan to get the power to the wheels. I would recommend that you review the diagrams with them to see if their plans are at all feasible.

3. Discuss materials with the students. Anything is possible. I have seen copious amounts of string, cardboard, styrofoam, plywood, plastic, and wire hangers used for the bodies, and anything round (or almost) for the wheels, including plastic snap-on can lids and old phonograph records. It is important to note that materials have very little to do with the outcome of the project and that the most successful have always been of the "home grown" variety. About the only thing that might have to be purchased is a mousetrap, which is readily available in most grocery or hardware stores.

4. Following is a diagram of a prototype mousetrap car that is very successful. You may use your discretion on how you want to use it with students because a pattern tends to limit the scope of creativity.

5. Happy mousetrapping!

Mousetrap Car Design Sheet

Engineer _____

Design Date _____

This sheet is provided for the design of your mousetrap car. Make your sketches. Label all of the parts and make some notes about what you think you will be using for materials. Consult with the Head Engineer before you begin construction.

The Mousetrap Car: A Prototype

The diagram below is of a very conventional mousetrap car. It uses two axles and four wheels. The wheels on the front axle(s) are not attached and turn easily. The rear axle is attached to the wheels so that the energy from the mousetrap spring can be used to turn the wheels. Remember, you are not limited to this design whatsoever. Great inventors don't keep doing things the same way others do.

String

Wire

4
THINGS THAT SLIDE

Inclined planes! It's hard to believe, but we are on our way home already. See, this simple machines stuff wasn't so hard after all. Just a few short activities ago we were teaching our students that simple machines help us do work by trading force for distance; now we are on the last family of simple machines!

Inclined planes can be fragmented into about four subgroups if you wish. The groups are typically: inclined planes, moving inclined planes, screws, and wedges. For our purposes, humor me, and pretend that they are all basically the same ... because they are. Whenever you throw a board on a step a little higher or lower than you are so that it is easier to walk or move a heavy or awkward object that you do not want to lift, you have created an inclined plane. Now pretend that you could take that board and mold it as if it were made of modeling clay so that you could make your ramp curve around a corner as it rises. Hmmmm, this is starting to sound a lot like a spiral staircase, isn't it? Now, keep this spiral going up for three or four complete turns. If you could stand off to the side and look at it, it would look like the threads on a giant bolt! Aha! A screw!

As you stand back and look at the basic shape of the inclined plane, you will see that the comparisons hold true for the remaining subgroups. Basically, the outline of the inclined plane is a triangle with the ground as one side, the plane as the second side, and the height from the ground to the top of the plane as the third side. As you keep this triangular shape in your mind, tip it up on the point and have it split a log as you make the pieces small enough to fit into the fireplace. Aha! A moving inclined plane or a wedge. If the points of two inclined planes were placed toward each other and an object placed between them, the planes could be forced together at the same time to cut the object in two. Examples of this situation would be a pair of scissors cutting a piece of paper or a pair of wire cutters cutting a wire.

In its basic form as an inclined plane, we often refer to it as a ramp. The purpose of a ramp is to overcome the pull of gravity. Gravity is the force that pulls objects toward the center of the earth. The greater the mass of the object, the heavier it feels to us and the harder it is to overcome the force of gravity. The inclined plane supports a portion of the weight of the object. The steeper the slope of the ramp, the less pull of gravity it overcomes. Therefore, you are only overcoming the friction between the ramp and the object as well as the portion of the pull of gravity absorbed by the ramp.

Simple machines help us do work by trading force for distance. The longer the ramp and the more shallow the slope, the easier it will be to move the object using an inclined plane. You will need to travel a greater distance with the object you are trying to move, but the force required will be significantly less. When we discuss work a little later on, you will find that the amount of "work" is the same, it was just easier to do the job.

Enough of this. This concept will become much simpler after we work through some activities.

more trucks

MAIN IDEA: An inclined plane is a sloped surface.

An inclined plane helps us do work by trading force for distance.

The steeper the slope, the more force it takes to move an object along an inclined plane.

PROCESS SKILLS: Interpreting data
Measuring
Predicting

MATERIALS:
Books
Desks or boards
Masses
Spring scales
Toy trucks or cars

TIME: 30-45 minutes

PROCEDURE:
1. Earlier, when you were finding out about wheels and axles, you used toy trucks or cars and put a mass in the vehicle to find out how much the wheel and axle assisted in reducing the amount of force it takes to move an object. You will be setting this experiment up in much the same way, except that you will be varying the angle or slope on which the truck will travel.

2. Attach the spring scale to the truck and mass and find out the combined weight of the pair by lifting the spring scale. Record the weight on the activity sheet titled "more trucks."

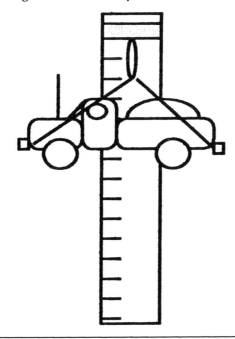

3. Move the truck and mass across the board or surface of the desk with it in a horizontal position. Record the information.

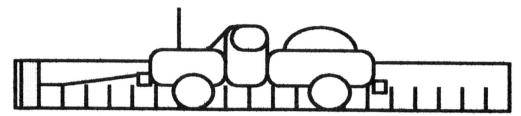

4. Now place a book under one end of the board or legs of the desk and move the truck up the ramp. Record the results.

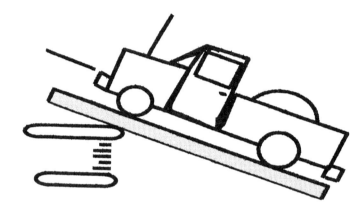

5. Repeat the procedure, adding more books under the end of the inclined plane and testing the force it takes to move the truck up the ramp.

6. Discuss the results. As you steepen the slope or incline of the plane, you should experience that it takes more force to do the job. As the slope increases, the ramp is absorbing less and less of the pull of gravity and you are having to do more and more of the lifting. (It's one of those physics/vectors things again.)

    An alternative to using trucks or cars if you cannot come up with a reasonable number for use with your class is to use that old science text instead!

1. Take about 18 inches of string or so and tie it into a loop.

2. Open the book to the approximate middle and insert the loop into the book. Close the book. (Phew! I thought I was going to have to read it!)

3. Open a paper clip into a C shape and attach it to the loop of string. Attach your spring scale to the clip and progress through the procedures that you would have done with the toy trucks. You could also do this activity as a reteach of the prior activity.

Name _____

Date _____

more trucks

What is the combined weight of your truck and mass? _____ units

Number of books under the end of your inclined plane	How much force do you think it will take to pull/push your vehicle up the ramp?	How much force did it take to move your vehicle up the ramp?

Describe what you see happening as the number of books increases under the ramp. _____

levitating the teacher

MAIN IDEA: An inclined plane is any surface that slopes.

An inclined plane can be fixed or moving.

An inclined plane can be used to lift a weight.

PROCESS SKILLS: Inferring
Interpreting data
Measuring
Predicting

MATERIALS:
Hammer
Shingles, shakes, or wedges cut from a piece of hardwood
2 tables or desks

TIME: 20-30 minutes

PROCEDURE:

1. Stand a table in a normal position in the middle of the room.

2. Turn a second table over and set it on top of the first table.

3. Between the two table surfaces place the inclined planes (shingles, shakes, or hardwood wedges) as evenly spaced as possible.

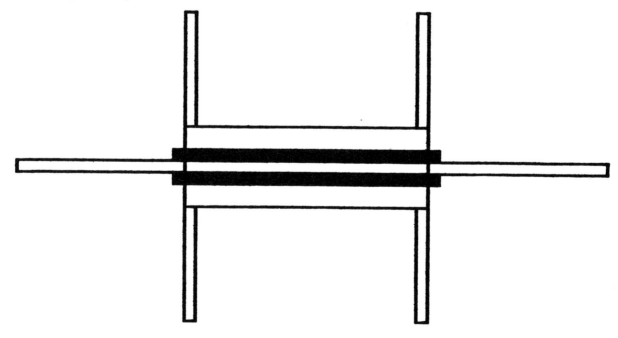

4. Tell the students that you will be sitting in the middle of the table on top. Individuals will be tapping on the ends of the wedges with the hammer. Ask them the following:

   a. What do you think will happen?

   b. How much force do you think it will take to lift the teacher?

   c. How far do you think I will be lifted with each tap of the hammer?

   These predictions will help them to focus their attention on the process and provide some investment into their observations.

5. Have the students take turns measuring how far you are lifted at each tap (mm or cm on the metric side of their rulers would be easiest to use). They should measure on all 4 sides of the table (if it is rectangular). They should observe that the table doesn't lift at all on the side opposite the wedge, lifts less on the sides adjacent to the wedge, and lifts the most on the side of the wedge.

6. Each student should experience the process of how much or how little force it takes to lift you with the hammer.

7. Discuss their observations.

8. If several hammers and a supply of wedges are available, you could do this as smaller groups after the class demonstration.

wisecrackers

MAIN IDEA: An inclined plane is any surface that is sloped.

An inclined plane can be fixed or moving.

The slope of the inclined plane determines the amount of force required to move an object.

PROCESS SKILLS: Inferring
Interpreting data
Measuring
Predicting

MATERIALS:
Boards with holes about 2 inches apart
Bolts with matching nuts—3/8 inch is a good size
The bolts should be around 4 inches long or a little longer; obtain sets that have both "coarse" and "fine" threads. The person at the hardware store should be happy to help you: Just tell him or her that it is for a science project and he or she won't try and get too technical with you. (Remember, no one understands science!)
Walnuts or other hard nuts in the shell
Washers
Wrenches to fit the bolts and nuts (not the walnuts!)

TIME: 30 minutes

PROCEDURE:
1. Acquire some sets of 2 boards with holes drilled about 2 inches apart. If you are building the sets, I would recommend that the boards be at least 6 inches square.

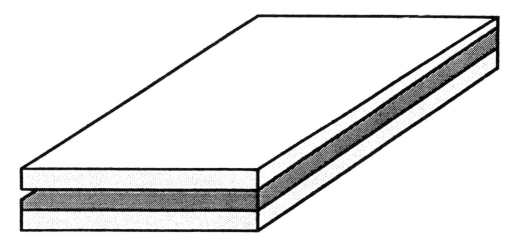

---

2. Place 2 boards on top of each other and drill two holes that are about 2 inches apart. The holes should be large enough, 1/2 inch, to accommodate the bolts without them binding in the holes.

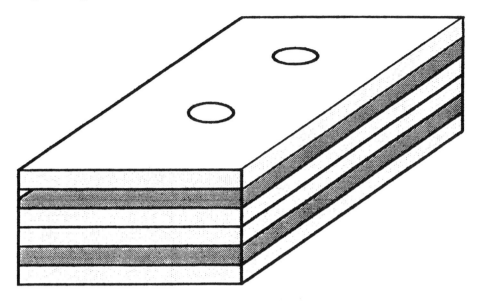

3. Place a washer on a coarse and a fine threaded bolt and feed the bolts down through the holes in the board. Then put on a second washer and nut on the bolts.

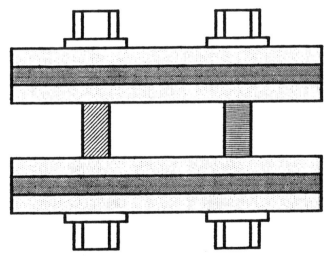

4. Have the students hold onto a walnut or other hardshell nut and let them try to crush it by squeezing it in their fist. Then, insert the nut between the bolts. Twist the nuts on the bolts with your fingers until they are snug (see page 108).

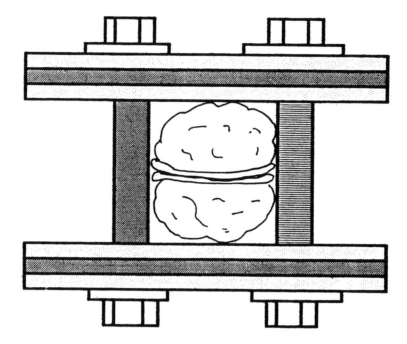

5. Using a wrench, twist the bolt and nut combination until the nut cracks. Try with the coarse thread first, then again with the fine thread and a new nut. The students should make observations about:

   a. how many turns it takes to crack the nut, and

   b. how much force was needed to turn the wrench with both kinds of threads.

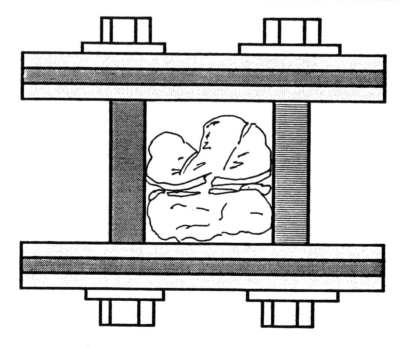

6. Discuss the observations. The students should notice that it takes fewer turns with the coarse thread to crack the nut, but that it requires measurably more force. This should be painfully obvious now, because "simple machines help us do work by trading force for distance."

cut ups

MAIN IDEA: An inclined plane is any sloped surface.

An inclined plane can be fixed or moving.

A moving inclined plane can be used to reduce the force necessary to do a job.

PROCESS SKILL: Interpreting data

MATERIALS:

Copper wire, 14 gauge or larger
Wire cutters

TIME: 15 minutes

The purpose of this activity is to show the path of a moving inclined plane and how it can be used to do a useful job.

PROCEDURE:

1. Strip several short sections of copper wire.

2. Ask the students to predict what the shape of the end of the wire will be when you cut it with the wire cutters. Most will probably anticipate that the wire will be cut cleanly across at right angles to the length of the wire. The resulting cuts will actually be at the same angle as the angle of the cutters on the wire-cutting pliers. The cutters are not only entering the wire, but separating it as well.

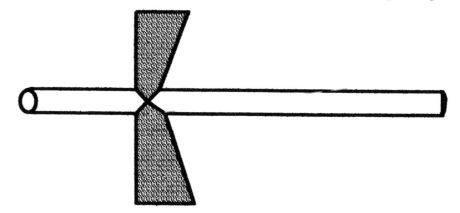

3. Let the students cut sections of the wire themselves to verify the cutting angle and the process.

threads

MAIN IDEA: An inclined plane is any sloped surface.

The slope of inclined planes varies.

Threads of a bolt or screw are curving inclined planes.

PROCESS SKILLS: Interpreting data
Predicting

MATERIALS:
Paper scraps
Pencils
Scissors

TIME: 15-20 minutes

PROCEDURE:

1. Have the students collect a number of old pieces of scrap paper.

2. From any corner of the paper, cut across to the opposite side. This should give them a right triangle. Have them cut several right triangles from their scraps of paper.

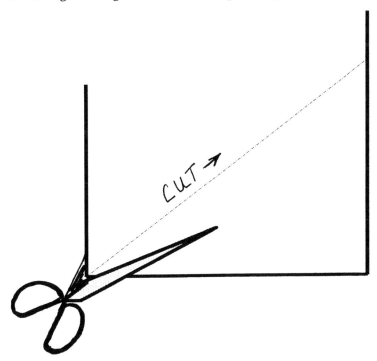

3. Place the right angle of the triangle next to the eraser of the pencil and either adjacent side along the pencil. Then wrap the paper around the pencil until it runs out. Compare the edge that wraps around the pencil as it wraps upward. Draw the comparison with the threads on a screw or bolt.

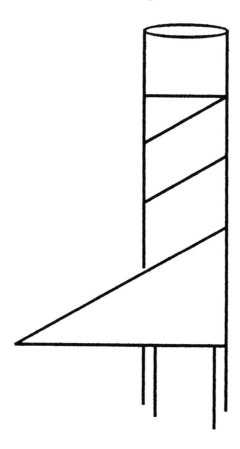

more threads

MAIN IDEA: An inclined plane is any sloped surface.

The slope of inclined planes varies.

Threads of a bolt or screw are curving inclined planes.

PROCESS SKILLS: Interpreting data
Predicting

MATERIALS:
Screwdrivers
Screws, in a variety of sizes and threads—2 to 5 depending on availability
(Hardware stores typically sell bulk screws at a penny or two apiece.)
Wood scraps
A hammer and nail
(Sometimes the screws are hard to start for kids; if you make a small hole by hitting a nail once with the hammer and pulling it out with your hands, the screws usually start quite easily.)

TIME: 30 minutes

PROCEDURE:

1. Pass out screws, a screwdriver, and a block of wood to each group.

2. Ask them to lay the screws out on the table in the order in which they think the screws will be easiest to hardest to drive into the wood with the screwdrivers.

3. Ask them to share why they chose the order that they did.

4. Have them drive the screws into the block of wood.

5. Compare their predictions concerning which was actually easiest to hardest.

6. If each group has the same variety of screws, you can compare the results to do something very scientific called verifying your data.

5
THINGS THAT RUB

"Say, hey, Ralphie, what's the rub?" That's one of those kind of sayings that happens to stick in your mind when you have a name like mine. I have a hard time with the citations for this kind of trivia, but it seems like a very appropriate introduction for the topic of friction.

Friction occurs when two objects rub together. The amount of friction that is created is determined by the amount and texture of the surfaces that are rubbing together and how hard they are rubbing together. The by-product of friction is always heat, and usually wear or fatigue of the surfaces.

This brings us to good friction and bad friction. Now wait a minute, if the by-product of friction is heat and wear, how can there be good friction? Good friction is often called traction. When the roads are icy or wet, our tires have a tendency to slip or skid because there is not enough friction between the tires and the road. Lack of friction is what I experience whenever I try to roller skate or ice skate! There is a severe tendency to experience a lot of movement back and forth without moving ahead. Good friction is what we are looking for when we dry our hands just before we try to take the lid off the new pickle or jam jar. It's why we put a rubber band around the top of the jar before trying to loosen the lid.

Bad friction is when two moving objects rub together, causing permanent damage to the moving parts. That's why oil companies run commercials that claim their products can prevent excessive engine wear through their superior lubricating ability. This is one of those half-full or half-empty arguments because, if friction and abrasion didn't occur, then sandpaper would not serve the purpose for which it was intended.

For our study of simple machines, we will say that friction occurs when two objects rub together. Its presence can be useful or can require more force to conduct a task if it has to be overcome. Greater friction occurs when surface area increases and the pressure holding the two surfaces together increases.

rub-a-dub-dub

MAIN IDEA: Friction occurs when two objects rub together.

Friction increases when there is greater surface area or pressure.

PROCESS SKILLS: Inferring
Interpreting data

MATERIALS:
Two hands each

TIME: 5 minutes

The following is a useful anticipatory set when introducing friction activities with students.

PROCEDURE:
1. Ask the students to hold their hands out in front of themselves.

2. Have them rub their hands gently together. Ask what they feel.

3. Now have them rub their hands harder. What changes in sensation do they feel?

4. Now have the students rub their hands together as fast as they can. The reaction is almost immediate. Through discussion you should be able to determine with the group that the elements of friction are two objects that rub together, and that the by-product is heat.

5. Next, repeat the activity, but have the students rub only the tips of their index fingers together. They will be able to experience the sensation of friction, but they will not be able to produce the heat they did when they were rubbing the palms of their hands together. From your discussion you should be able to compare the two incidents and find that the difference is the amount of surface area of the fingertips compared to the palms of the hands.

easy slider

MAIN IDEA: Friction occurs when two objects rub together.

Friction increases when surface area increases, texture roughens, and pressure increases.

PROCESS SKILLS: Interpreting data
Measuring
Predicting

MATERIALS:
Small carpet squares
Cooking oil
Cornstarch
Masking tape
Masses
Plastic wrap
Sandpaper
Spring scale
Drinking straws
Waxed paper

TIME: 45 minutes

The activity works well if students can work in groups of two.

PROCEDURE:

1. Give each group a spring scale, mass, and about a foot of masking tape.

2. Refer the students to the activity sheet titled "easy slider." Indicate that they will be recording all of their observations on that sheet and that before they conduct any trial they should record a prediction on the sheet.

3. Ask them to record the weight of their masses on the activity sheet. Then place the mass on the table and attach the spring scale. Each group should record their prediction on how much force it is going to take to slide the mass across the tabletop.

4. Before they complete the trial, they should record a word that describes the texture of the surface across which they will be sliding the mass. Brainstorm a list of words that can be considered as texture words to expand their vocabulary. Words like *rough*, *coarse*, *gritty*, and *bumpy* should be included rather than *soft* or *hard*.

5. Finally, slide the mass across the tabletop and record the force that is required.

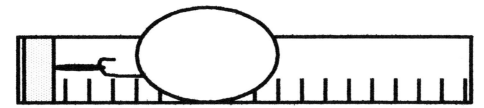

6. Pass out the carpet squares and repeat the steps as before for predicting force and describing texture. Place the carpet fuzzy side down on the table. Then, put a little circle of tape on the back of the carpet and attach the mass to the tape. Hook the spring scale to the mass and pull the assembly across the tabletop.

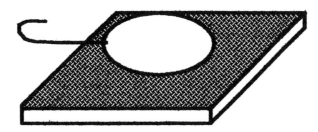

7. Turn the carpet square over and repeat the process. The back of the carpet square provides a completely different texture to move across the table. Record the results on the activity sheet.

8. Collect the carpet squares and replace them with a small square of sandpaper. Attach the sandpaper to the mass with masking tape, record the prediction and texture on the activity sheet, and complete the trial.

9. Pass out about a dozen drinking straws to each group. Lay them parallel to and touching each other. Place the mass on the bed of straws and push it along the tabletop.

10. Place a square of waxed paper on the tabletop. Attach the 4 corners to the table with small pieces of masking tape. Slide the mass across the waxed surfae, recording the results.

11. Sprinkle cornstarch on the waxed paper. The students should feel the texture of the cornstarch between their fingers before conducting the trial. When this trial is completed, roll up the waxed paper and cornstarch and dispose of it in the trash.

12. Repeat the activity using plastic wrap. The results should be surprising!

13.   With the plastic wrap still in place, put a small quantity of cooking oil on the wrap for the students. Then have them repeat the trial, predicting, determining the texture, and recording the results.

14.   Discuss the results.

A lot is happening in this experiment. The variables are changing quite rapidly, and it is important to keep track of them for each of the trials. First, and most important, the table is supporting the mass; thus the amount of pressure is consistent for each of the trials because the pull of gravity is always the same on the mass. With the mass, the carpet squares, the sandpaper, and the waxed paper, the amount of force to move the mass across the table is a measure of the friction between the two surfaces.

The straws are unique because they create a phenomenon known as rolling friction. Friction is a function of texture and surface area. When you feel the straws, they feel "bumpy." However, this is not a rough or bumpy texture. The point of contact of the mass to the straws and the straws to the table is very small. Therefore, the surface area is very limited, reducing the friction. Also, the surface of any one straw is very smooth and very little friction occurs between smooth surfaces.

The cornstarch and cooking oil are lubricants. Lubricants work by filling in all of the rough or irregular surfaces, thus creating smooth surfaces that allow objects to slide past without much resistance.

And then there is the plastic wrap. Oh, my! It seems to have a very smooth surface and thus should have very little friction. Yet is turns out to require one of the highest amounts of force necessary to move the mass across it in the experiment. Static cling! Have you ever wondered why plastic wrap works? There are tremendous amounts of static charges held within plastic wrap. When the charged plastic wrap comes in contact with a neutral surface, it clings and the plastic "flows" into all of those hard-to-see irregular surfaces. So, instead of the plastic wrap creating a smooth, slippery surface, it actually turns into a clingy, grabby surface, creating a lot of friction.

Name _____
Date _____

——— easy slider ———

What is the weight of your mass? _____ units

What object are you testing?	What is a word that describes its texture?	How much force do you think it will take to move the mass?	How much force did it take to move the mass?

Describe what you found out about the way a mass moves across different surfaces. Did things turn out the way you thought they would? Why or why not? _____

_____

_____

_____

_____

_____

just warmin' up

MAIN IDEA: Friction occurs when two objects rub together.

Friction increases as pressure and surface area increase.

PROCESS SKILLS: Inferring
Measuring
Observing
Predicting

MATERIALS:
Block of wood
Large dowel
Thermometers with exposed bulb

TIME: 15-20 minutes

These are two simple activities that students can do to observe the by-products of friction: heat and fatigue (wear) of materials.

PROCEDURE:
1. Have the students move their chairs out from under their desks.

2. Place the bulb of their thermometers on the garment covering their thigh. Wait about one minute and record the temperature on a piece of paper.

3. Have them place their hands, palms down, on their thighs, press firmly and rub back and forth as fast and hard as they can.

4. As quickly as possible, place the bulb of the thermometer on the area that experienced the friction. Record the temperature on the same piece of paper.

5. Compare and discuss the results. Ask:

   a. What did you feel?

   b. What do you see happening to the palms of your hands?

   c. Was there a change in temperature? How much?

   d. How do you account for the change or lack of it when your hands feel so warm?

6. Take a dowel about 6 inches long and sharpen the end of it. For each dowel you should have a small block of wood with a slight depression in the middle.

7. Record observations about the appearance of the depression in the block and the end of the dowel, including the temperature of the depression in the block of wood. Discuss what kinds of changes they might anticipate they will observe (color, temperature, smell, texture of the dowel and block).

8. Place the point of the dowel down into the depression of the block and hold the dowel between the palms with the fingers fully extended.

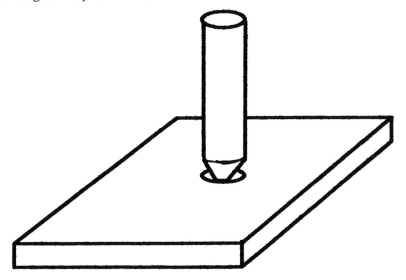

9. Rub your palms back and forth as fast as you can.

10. Quickly record any temperature changes in the depression of the block of wood. Record and compare the results.

11. Observe the end of the dowel and the depression in the block of wood. Record and discuss the observations. Ask:

   a. What changes did you observe?

   b. How can you account for some of those changes?

   c. Why did the end of the dowel and the hole in the block of wood turn brown?

slip slidin' away (just warmin' up—the sequel)

MAIN IDEA: Friction occurs when two objects rub together.

Lubricants reduce friction.

Lubricants work by filling in small spaces to remove texture, to lessen contact between surfaces, and to remove heat (a by-product of friction).

PROCESS SKILLS: Inferring
Observing
Predicting

MATERIALS:
Blocks of wood
Dowels
Liquid soap
Thermometers with exposed bulbs

TIME: 15-20 minutes

The following activities are an excellent follow-up to the previous exercise. They demonstrate the effect that a lubricant will have on friction.

PROCEDURE:

1. Have the students hold their hands out in front of themselves with their palms up.

2. Drop a dollop of liquid soap on one palm. Ask them to fold their hands together once or twice as if they were washing their hands.

3. Holding their hands out with palms together, they should press firmly and rub their hands back and forth together as fast as they can. Discuss what they feel. Compare it to when they rubbed their hands together dry in the "rub-a-dub-dub" activity and on their thighs in the "just warmin' up" activity.

4. Now, repeat the activity with the sharpened dowel and the block of wood. This time, however, place several drops of liquid soap in the depression in the block of wood, take the temperature of the depression, and then spin the dowel rapidly in the depression.

5. After the dowel has been spun for a minute or 2, record the temperature and observe any changes you might find in the depression and on the end of the dowel.

6

THINGS THAT WORK

Mechanical advantage is the amount of effort that a simple machine supplies in doing work. It is a mathematical calculation based on the relationship of the amount of force you apply compared to the amount of resistance there is to that force. Simply stated, it is how much the machine helps you do work by trading force for distance.

Mechanical advantage is often found in a sentence like: "It was twice as easy when I used the lever" or "I lifted three times as much as I normally could have when I used the block and tackle" or "I would never have been able to make it up that hill if I had not had that tenth gear on my bike."

When thinking about simple machines and trying to explain them in terms of mechanical advantage it is sometimes helpful if you think of the job that you might be trying to do if you did not have the machine. For example, you might want to place a 100-pound rock up onto a small terrace in your garden. Most of us wouldn't or shouldn't try to do the job by stooping over to lift the rock. And, most important, if we only have the capacity to lift, say, 50 pounds, somehow we are going to have to increase our force by a factor of two or make a trip to the chiropractor. The simple machine chosen to assist us must have the potential for a mechanical advantage of two or be able to magnify our force by two to do the job. If there is a lever (old board) nearby and another smaller rock, we could stick the small rock next to the one we want to lift and slide the end of the board under the big rock. If the distance between the big rock and the little rock (remember fulcrum?) is twice the distance from the little rock to you, you should be able to lift the big rock.

However, if a second rock is not around to use as a fulcrum, you could use the board as an inclined plane. Lay one end of the board on the terrace and the other end next to the terrace. If the rise (height of the terrace) is half of the run (distance of the rock from the terrace), then you have enough force to roll the rock up the inclined plane. The mechanical advantage would be two.

As you introduce this discussion and analysis to your students, it is probably best if you keep the number relationships in whole numbers. If you divide, especially around grade four, the remainders will only cause unnecessary confusion and you will probably lose the point that you were trying to make by getting lost in math. Try not to make things harder than they need to be for you or for your students. The point is that whole number relationships or ratios can be meaningful. The mechanical advantage ratio of a lever at 3.65784987646 to 1 loses something in the translation, but three times easier even I can understand!

In the following section are two kinds of approaches to the discussion of mechanical advantage. The first approach features activities or participatory demonstrations. We all have the anonymous Chinese proverb committed to memory so we won't dwell on the value of doing in relation to learning. The second approach will show you how to mathematically calculate mechanical advantage for two prior activities. If you like using the mathematical analysis, I would highly encourage you to do so to extend any of the activities that you find in this volume.

We are not quite done yet, though. You will come across some mathematical calculations where you will find negative numbers, or an inability to divide the force applied into the amount of force that it takes to overcome the resistance of the object without the use of a simple machine. This is not too uncommon. Think back to the third-class levers. It always took more force to lift the mass with the lever than it did without it. The construction of this kind of lever was not for the reduction of force but rather to provide the ability to reach.

Hint: Watch your students' eyes! You can always tell when you are going out on a limb with your explanations!

For the mathematical calculations, no matter the simple machine, always use the following formula:

$$\text{Mechanical Advantage (MA)} = \frac{\text{Force needed without the simple machine}}{\text{Force needed with the simple machine}}$$

Example: A stranger lifted a huge rock weighing 500 pounds by standing on the end of a lever. When the stranger was asked to stand on a scale, the meter registered 100 pounds. How much mechanical advantage did the lever afford the stranger?

$$\frac{\text{Force without the machine}}{\text{Force with the machine}} = \frac{500 \text{ lbs.}}{100 \text{ lbs.}} \quad MA = 5$$

Conclusion: The stranger's body weight was magnified five times.

an uplifting experience

MAIN IDEA: Mechanical advantage is how much a simple machine will help you to perform a task. It is most easily expressed as a whole number ratio.

PROCESS SKILLS: Inferring
Predicting

MATERIALS:
Meter stick
Teacher and student
2 desks

TIME: 10 minutes

PROCEDURE:

1. Choose a reasonably sized student. Stand next to that person and ask the group to predict how many times heavier the larger is than the smaller. This, of course, will take a couple of minutes to travel from the ridiculous to the sublime.

2. Have the heavier person sit on one of the desks. Place the second desk a few inches away from the first.

3. Place the meter stick (usually made of a better grade of hardwood than yardsticks) on the edge (NOT FLAT!) so that the end of the meter stick hooks under the edge of the desk. The meter stick should cross the edge of the second desk.

4. The person on the ground should grasp the end of the meter stick and apply pressure. The person on the desk and the desk should easily lift off the ground an inch or 2.

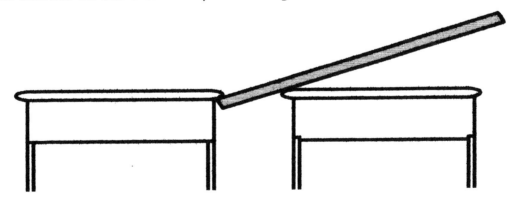

---

going up?

MAIN IDEA: Mechanical advantage is how much a simple machine will help us do a job.

PROCESS SKILLS: Interpreting data
Measuring
Predicting

MATERIALS:
An old rope block and tackle
(It is amazing how many there are around if you just put out the call to your students and their families. The last one I acquired was a gift from a home in downtown Seattle.)
Basketball hoop
Large dowel or broom handle
Or, a "come-along" (a pulley system consisting of pulleys, a gear, and a lever)

TIME: 15-30 minutes

PROCEDURE:
1. Attach the block and tackle to the base of a basketball hoop on the playground or in the gym.

2. Demonstrate how to work the block and tackle or problem solve it with your students.

3. Place the dowel in the bottom of the bottom pulley and stand with one foot on either side of the pulley. Ask the students to predict how many of them it will take to lift you or one of their classmates off the ground.

4. Allow for experimenting on how few it will take to do the lifting, or what combinations will be able to do the job. Estimate how much mechanical advantage there is in the block and tackle.

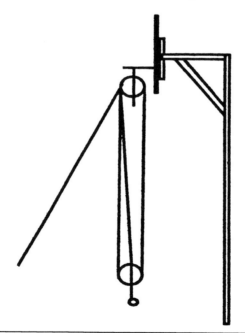

calculating mechanical advantage

MAIN IDEA: Mechanical advantage is the amount of effort that a machine contributes to a job. Mechanical advantage can be calculated mathematically.

PROCESS SKILLS: Interpreting data
Measuring

MATERIALS:
Lever
Masses
Spring scale
Windmill (constructed from an earlier activity)

TIME: 30-60 minutes

PROCEDURE:
1. Review the "first-class levers" activity procedure.

2. Have the students repeat the procedure and quickly collect the data with the varying fulcrum distances.

3. Discuss the concept of mechanical advantage, that is, to what degree a machine is helping you perform a task.

4. Show the students how to calculate the mechanical advantage by dividing the force it takes to do the job using the simple machine *into* the amount of force it takes to lift the object without using a simple or complex machine.

$$MA = \frac{\text{Force it takes without the machine}}{\text{Force it takes with the machine}}$$

The answer that comes from this division problem seems to be most meaningful for elementary students if it is rounded off to a whole number and then placed in a cloze statement:

"With the machine I used it was _____ times easier to do the job."

(Example is on page 128.)

Example: A stranger used a first-class lever 20 feet long to lift a heavy rock from one level of a terraced garden to the next. The stranger found the following when the rock being used for a fulcrum was moved closer and farther from the heavy rock.

Weight of the rock was ___100___ pounds.

Fulcrum distance	0'	4'	8'	10'	12'	14'
	5 lbs.	20 lbs.	80 lbs.	100 lbs.	120 lbs.	200 lbs.

MA 0' = 100/5 = 20

MA 4' = 100/20 = 5

MA 8' = 100/80 = 1.25 or just about 1

(Remember what we were going to do with the remainders? If you are doing this activity in grade five or above, I would certainly hold the students to the remainders and have them make a graph of the mechanical advantage, probably on the same grid as the force/fulcrum distance that you used for interpreting the graph for the first-class levers. You will see that it is an inverse proportion; that is, as the force curve is going up in relation to the fulcrum distance, the mechanical advantage is going down.)

MA 10' = 100/100 = 1

(Here is a good point to stop and review the very first lesson that we have all learned so well: "Simple machines help us do work by trading force for distance." With a 20-foot-long lever and the fulcrum at the midpoint, the force and the mass travel the same distance in opposite directions. Therefore, there is no mechanical advantage. The number 1 in mathematics and science is usually a constant, and here again it is true.)

MA 12' = 100/120 = .8

(Here there is no useful mechanical advantage because it is taking more force to lift the rock with the machine than without the lever.)

MA 14' = 100/200 = .5

(Ucky! Now it is taking twice as much force to lift the rock, or you are only getting one-half out of the machine what you put into it. Not a very good deal unless all you want to do is change directions or you have unlimited force at your disposal.)

There is always a difference between theoretical and actual mechanical advantage. The difference can usually be accounted for by friction, which causes energy loss in the forms of heat and wear. Let's use the example of the windmill that you built earlier. It is a good example to use with students because it will help them to estimate how much they might be able to lift under ideal conditions.

This is one example on which you will be able to pull out all of the stops or else take the easy way out! Let's try both, and you choose which one you might like to try based on your comfort level at this point and the level of your students' mathematical training. Hang on, here we go!

Example: You have just constructed a windmill. The straw that you used to pick up the string on has a diameter of one-half inch (1/2"). The distance across the vanes at the farthest point is 6 inches (6"). If you look at the windmill from the side, the vanes roughly resemble the spokes of a wheel, therefore, we are going to imagine we are looking at a circle (because we are!).

The Theoretical Mechanical Advantage (TMA) is calculated by comparing the circumference of the straw to the circumference of the circle described by the vanes of the windmill. The outer edge of the vane travels in a circular path, and using the force-for-distance reason for simple machines helping us, we need to find how many times farther the vane travels than the straw.

The hard way:

$$TMA = \frac{\text{Circumference of the vanes} = \pi D = 3.14 \times 6" = 18.84"}{\text{Circumference of the straw} = \pi D = 3.14 \times 1/2" = 1.57"} = 12$$

Therefore, the TMA is 12, or the windmill should be able to pick up 12 times as much weight as the wind from the hair dryer could hold up by itself.

The easy way:

Let's take a quick look at this now that we have been through the "long form." There is an easy way out. The first shortcut that you could take would be to round pi (π) off to three (3), because when we estimate the circumference of a circle, all we do is multiply the diameter by three (3). A circle is about 3 times as far around as it is across. So we could then simplify the problem to look like this:

$$TMA = \frac{\text{Circumference of the vanes} = \pi D = 3 \times 6" = 18}{\text{Circumference of the straw} = \pi D = 3 \times 1/2" = 1.5} = 12$$

(Hmmm, this answer is looking familiar!)

Now to make it really easy (why didn't he tell us this in the first place?)! By the way, this drives my students nuts, because I do it to them all of the time. It has to do with level of understanding. If you don't know why a shortcut works, then it has no universal application value. Anyway, if you look at the 3/3 in the problem, then you should see that it can be renamed in lowest terms as 1, which is the identity element in multiplication. (So, that's why we had to do identity elements in "Mathematics Education for the Elementary" when we went to school.) Therefore,

$$TMA = \frac{1 \times 6}{1/2} = 12 \quad \text{(Now this is getting to where I can understand it!)}$$

Let's make the quantum leap now that we understand how this works!

$$TMA = \frac{\text{diameter of the big circle} \quad 6}{\text{diameter of the little circle} = 1/2} = 12$$

No matter how you figure it, the mechanical advantage of the windmill is 12 or in the cloze sentence: "I can pick up __12__ times as much weight using the windmill."

In the interest of saving a few trees, there will be no further adaptations of the activities here for mechanical advantage. Almost all of the activities in this book could easily be adapted for a follow-up activity on mechanical advantage, and I would recommend doing so.

7
THINGS TO HANG ON THE WALL

A SIMPLE BULLETIN BOARD

Just for fun, sometime, ask the students what was on the beautifully planned, educationally sound bulletin board that you just replaced. Sadly, the possibility exists that many will have no idea what was there in general or in detail.

There are several reasons for this. The first and most important is that many of us use classroom bulletin boards for information only. A second reason is that many classrooms present stimulus overload for students and tend to shut out the specific because of the overall effect.

It's hard to be critical of our own creations sometimes, so wander with me into a colleague's room and survey the damage there instead. In my experience, what I often see is many splashes of color and a tremendous amount of busy-ness (not to be confused with business). This, of course, comes from the excruciatingly painful far right-sidedness of my mental organization. My overall impression is a disarray of colors with little or no consideration for coordination. It seems an educational sin if you do not have every possible color of butcher paper from the rack up on your wall at the same time.

One year, in response to this, I went art deco. All bulletin boards were white background with black trim and black and purple letters. Color was generated by splashes of green from plants and framed art-works and student contributions on the bulletin boards themselves.

The key to this is the student contributions on the bulletin boards. The students knew what was there for two vital reasons. They were responsible for the content, and the bulletin boards were inter-active. As students made contributions to the boards, they were discussed. Here is how it works:

Frame a neutral-colored bulletin board. Try to have the background color complement the major color on either side. Then section the board into three parts. Cut out letters for "LEVER," "WHEEL AND AXLE," and "INCLINED PLANE." I was a little creative about how the letters were placed. The word *lever* had a triangle under the middle to simulate a fulcrum, the words *inclined plane* sloped down to one side, and the words *wheel and axle* were done in a circle. Then came the assignment. Each student was asked to bring in two pictures that represented each of the three groups of simple machines. As the pictures grew, so did the bulletin board. Each student had to report on his or her contribution and how it would apply to the section of the bulletin board.

There are always a few management kinds of things to think about, of course. When does one take the time for the sharing of the articles? There are always the few minutes before or after recess, or just before or after lunch, or the two minutes between the music specialist and ..., or as a beginning or clos-ing of the science activity for the day. How do you get the students to bring pictures? Bribe them. Actually, I use it as part of the evaluation process and add points for each picture that is contributed. Extra credit? Why not! And the whiners. "We can't get a newspaper ..." ad nauseum. They all get mail, and along with it an unending supply of junk catalogs. And all of them have pictures.

A helpful hint: If the students are having trouble finding things, show them how to look back-wards. If they are looking for something they will never find it. Get them to look at any picture, tell what they see in it, and then identify what a part of the picture will do for them. The loose-leaf flyers in the weekend editions to the newspaper are really good for this, especially if there is one for a store that sells tools, like Sears. You could even have a few old mail order catalogs laying around to help them out.

Another option is to do this as a class project. Take a science period and put the whole thing together with the class, including the sharing of the pictures.

A LEARNING CENTER

The following learning center activities are classified in two ways. The first is by the family of simple machines. The second is by the first six levels of Bloom's Taxonomy: knowledge, comprehension, application, analysis, synthesis, and evaluation.

To save space in this text, the shapes for the task cards have been provided. Duplicate the task cards and an appropriate number of each shape card. Glue the tasks onto the shape cards and attach the shapes to a backing such as railroad board. For durability, laminate the completed cards. If you do not have a laminating machine at your disposal, cover the cards with clear contact paper.

I prefer color coding the background cards. Choose six different colors to represent the taxonomical levels. The colors of the rainbow are nice, but any will do. The purpose of this is to help set the students up for your expectations. I usually ask each student to complete at least one of each shape and each color. This affords a student the opportunity to complete each level of the taxonomy and a representative from each family of simple machines.

On page 132 is a pattern for making the pockets for your learning center. Some prefer a tri-fold center that sits on a counter, but I have found it easiest to just use a single sheet of railroad board (22 x 28 inches) as the background and attach it to the wall. It saves a lot of reinforcing. Just fold the pockets and attach them to the background, let them dry overnight, slap on a few pictures and a creative title like "Simple Machines," and away you go. Actually, it is very becoming. (Shape cards begin on page 133.)

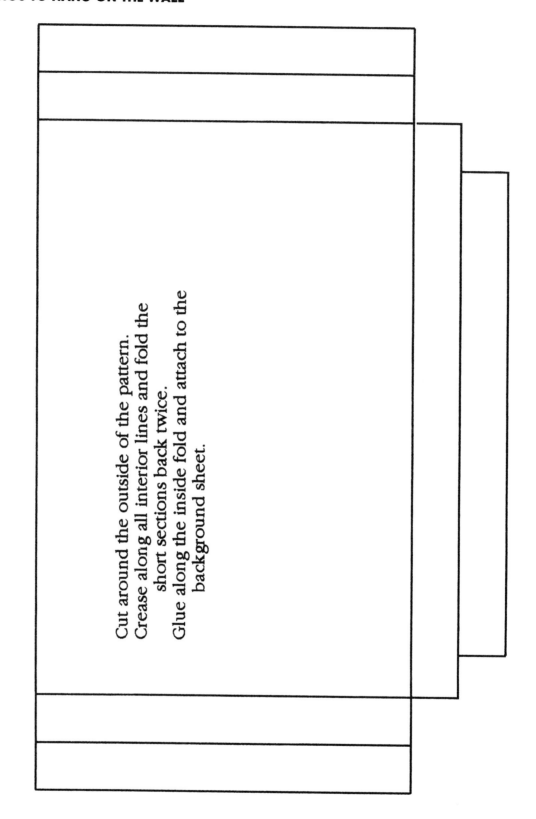

learning center pocket pattern

Cut around the outside of the pattern.
Crease along all interior lines and fold the short sections back twice.
Glue along the inside fold and attach to the background sheet.

LEARNING CENTER SHAPE CARDS

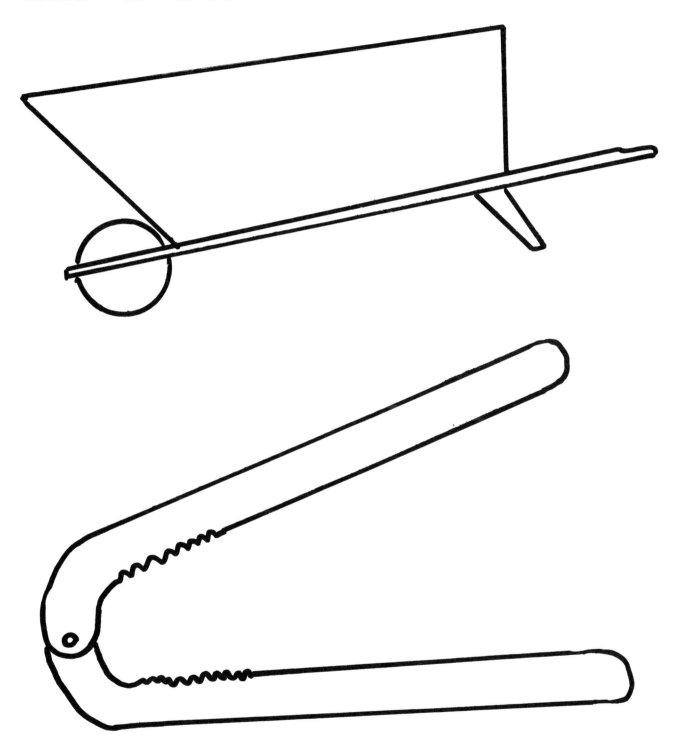

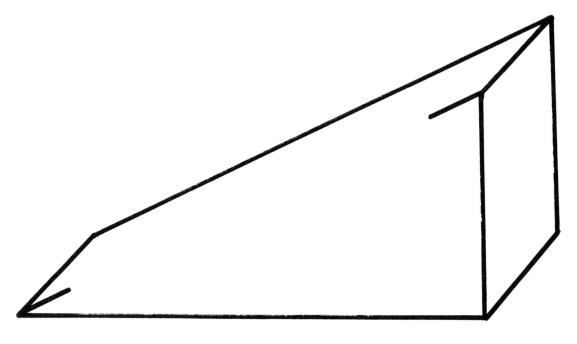

Levers

Draw a picture of a lever.

KNOWLEDGE

Make a poster of pictures of levers.

KNOWLEDGE

Make a fact file of information
about levers.

KNOWLEDGE

Draw and label the parts
of a lever.

KNOWLEDGE

Draw a diagram of a lever system
and label the parts.

COMPREHENSION

Find and identify pictures of
the three classes of levers.

COMPREHENSION

Make a diorama of a lever
being used to help do work.

COMPREHENSION

Make a list of 10 tools that can be
used as a lever.

COMPREHENSION

Make a chart for the classroom to show
others the three classes of
levers.

APPLICATION

Be a reporter and write a story
about a lever that you find being used
on the playground.

APPLICATION

Make a crossword puzzle using
words that are related to levers.

APPLICATION

Make a toy for a younger person
that uses a lever somewhere.

APPLICATION

Make a chart that compares the
similarities and differences of the
three classes of levers.

ANALYSIS

Interview the school custodian and
find out how he or she uses levers to
help do the job.

ANALYSIS

Make a filmstrip to
demonstrate to a classmate
how a lever works.

ANALYSIS

Make a questionnaire you would
use with your friends to find out
what they know about levers.

ANALYSIS

Make up a story or poem
in which levers are being used
to solve a problem.

SYNTHESIS

Create a new piece of playground
equipment that has a lever in it.
Draw a diagram and make up a parts list.

SYNTHESIS

Design a tool advertisement
for a tool that is a lever.

SYNTHESIS

Make a board game
about levers.

SYNTHESIS

If you are the engineer on a road
project and have to lift a heavy beam
up onto a bridge, which kind of lever
would you use and why?

EVALUATION

Make up an experiment to find out
which is the best kind of lever
to use.

EVALUATION

Find several different kinds of pliers
and decide which one would be the best
to do a job. Tell why you chose the
one you did.

EVALUATION

Describe the different kinds of levers
and tell why each is
important.

EVALUATION

Wheel and Axle

Write a short report on the
wheel and axle.

KNOWLEDGE

Collect 10 pictures of the wheel and axle
from magazines.

KNOWLEDGE

Read a short book in which you find that
that wheels and axles are used to do a job.

KNOWLEDGE

Make a mobile with pictures of the
wheel and axle.

KNOWLEDGE

Draw a cartoon in which a
wheel and axle is being used.

COMPREHENSION

Paint a picture in which a
wheel and axle is being used.

COMPREHENSION

Make a poster showing how fixed and
and free wheel and axles are used.

COMPREHENSION

Make a chart showing how
the wheel and axle help to do work.

COMPREHENSION

Make a rolling planter box for
your mom.

APPLICATION

Make a model of a vehicle that someone
could play with that has wheel and axles.

APPLICATION

Conduct a survey in a department store
to find out which kinds of
merchandise have a wheel and axle.

APPLICATION

Make a matching game in which
someone has to identify types of
wheel and axles.

APPLICATION

Make a diagram of a pencil sharpener
and show at least three
wheel and axles.

ANALYSIS

Explain why there are so many
different gears on a
bicycle sprocket.

ANALYSIS

Make a diagram of a block and tackle.
Describe what each part does and
calculate how much mechanical
advantage each pulley has.

ANALYSIS

Construct a cart with wheels. Find out
how much it reduces force when you roll
it across the floor. Change the size of
the wheels and try again.

ANALYSIS

In a story, tell how the wheel and axle
might be used on the moon 20 years
from now.

SYNTHESIS

Pretend that a pair of wheels could talk.
Create a cartoon strip
about one of their adventures.

SYNTHESIS

Write a short story that imagines
how the wheel and axle
were invented.

SYNTHESIS

Collect a whole bunch of old toy
cars and trucks and assemble a new
vehicle from the parts.

SYNTHESIS

Some bicycles have tall skinny tires,
and some have shorter wider tires.
Which are the best to use and
where would you use them?

EVALUATION

What is the best number of gears
to have on a bicycle and why?
Discuss this issue as a panel.

EVALUATION

You are responsible for the design of a
winch that will pull a large weight
up onto a trailer. How will you go
about choosing which size of spool will
be the best to use?

EVALUATION

There has been a lot of terrible weather
recently and the roads cannot stand
the normal amount of travel. As highway
commissioner, which vehicles are you
going to allow on the roads and why?

EVALUATION

Inclined Planes

Find out how inclined planes are
used in at least four different ways.

KNOWLEDGE

Make a list of at least six different
kinds of inclined planes.

KNOWLEDGE

Make a fact file about different
kinds of inclined planes.

KNOWLEDGE

Draw a picture of at least two
varieties of inclined planes.

KNOWLEDGE

Collect and display at least five
kitchen utensils that have
inclined planes.

COMPREHENSION

Make a board that displays
many different kinds of bolts or screws
screws to show inclined planes.

COMPREHENSION

Cut words out from a newspaper to
make three sentences about
inclined planes.

COMPREHENSION

Write an acrostic verse for
"INCLINED PLANE."

COMPREHENSION

Set up a demonstration for your class
to show how to split wood
with a wedge.

APPLICATION

Set up a test with your classmates to
show which kind of screw is easiest to
drive into a piece of wood.

APPLICATION

Offer to help build a ramp for a
disabled person.

APPLICATION

Show someone who is trying to lift
a heavy object how an inclined plane
can help him or her.

APPLICATION

Make a chart to demonstrate the
similarities and differences between
bolts and screws.

ANALYSIS

Talk to people to find out how they
use inclined planes
and why.

ANALYSIS

Construct a poster to show how
a wedge helps to do work by
trading force for distance.

ANALYSIS

Find a picture in a magazine. Look
carefully and circle any places an
inclined plane might be used.

ANALYSIS

Write a short report on how you
suppose that inclined planes will be
used in outer space.

SYNTHESIS

On the moon you only weigh one-sixth
of what you do on Earth. Going down
a slide might not be as much fun.
Make up a new game using inclined
planes.

SYNTHESIS

Make up a board game
that uses inclined planes.

SYNTHESIS

Write a myth like the Greeks did in
which there is an inclined plane.

SYNTHESIS

You have to make a choice between two bolts that are going to hold the wing on a large airliner. Are you going to use one with threads close together or far apart? Why?

EVALUATION

You are building a slide for the playground. How are you going to design it? Why?

EVALUATION

What is the most important kind of inclined plane? Why?

EVALUATION

In a debate, your team is asked to defend the statement "The inclined plane is the most important simple machine." Write your speech.

EVALUATION

□
8
THINGS THAT COME AT THE END

FINAL EVALUATION

The following evaluation is a "product-post unit" as described in the introduction. It gives the students the opportunity to diagram and demonstrate what they have learned in this experience with simple machines.

There needs to be some consideration for the success of this activity. The first is the final deadline that should be set by you for when the project is due. Reasonable time to finish is necessary as some students will put serious effort into this undertaking. My recommendation through experience is about two weeks. This allows the students to do a really good job. Our experience tells us that most will wait until the night before the deadline to do what needs to be done. So, if they are given a month, they will take a month.

Parent involvement is always an issue. I have some personal feelings about this, which you might consider. Most of the students that I encounter get little enough quality time as it is at home. Even though this is intended as a student project, sometimes the parents can't stand not being involved in a fun project. So, if the parent can work with the student, we have been able to provide an opportunity that would not occur otherwise. To minimize the effect that parent involvement can have on a project like this, a note home is often helpful. In the note it is easy to alert the parents of the expectancies of the project and let them know that they can assist the student only as a pair of hands. The student at all times must be the "brains" behind the operation. Most students have had little or no exposure to tools, and the parent's or parents' assistance can be very beneficial.

The grading rubrics should be relatively straightforward and outlined at the onset. The complex machine must contain at least two different simple machines used to provide mechanical advantage. This is an "A" or an "F" kind of a project for me, but you can construct any kind of grading scale you wish.

Be prepared to be amazed at the panorama of contraptions that will enter your domain! Whenever life gives you lemons, make lemonade. The "geospools" activity described in this book came from a student project. A student came in with a board with about 20 spools nailed to it and a single cord painfully entwined through the spools.... You couldn't have lifted a weight with a crane! But for me it was an aha! that extended our unit an extra two days!

the final product

Name _____

Date _____

Now is your chance to demonstrate to the world how much you have learned about simple machines by building a machine that will overwhelm whoever might be lucky enough to see it. All you have to do is to build a machine combining at least two simple machines to lift 8 pounds with as little force as possible. (8 pounds is what a gallon milk container weighs when it is full of water!) You will have the opportunity to demonstrate it to all who would see on _____.

Draw a diagram of your machine in the remaining space and label the machines and stuff that you will be using. Present this plan on "Machine Day."

THINGS WITH MEANING

GLOSSARY

abrasion   The wear shown on surfaces that rub together.

anticipatory set   A short activity designed to introduce a lesson and develop interest.

apparatus   Equipment that is set up in an experiment.

balance   A first-class lever that is used to weigh objects by putting an unknown on one side of the fulcrum and a known quantity of weight on the other.

block and tackle   A combination of fixed and movable pulleys used to lift heavy weights. The pulleys are the block and the ropes or lines are the tackle.

bolt   The combination of a cyclinder and an inclined plane. The slope of the inclined plane determines how close the threads are to each other.

calibrate   The process of assigning values to the marks or increments on any device that is used to measure.

cantilever   A lever that is suspended out over a space and anchored by a heavy weight on the other end.

catapult   A complex machine that is the combination of a wheel and axle and a third-class lever. It is used to launch projectiles.

classifying   A scientific process skill of grouping objects into groups determined by similar attributes.

complex machine   The combination of two or more simple machines.

crank   A lever that turns in a circle around a point that is used to wind up a rope or line.

customary   Standard units of measurement that are commonly used, like centimeters or pounds.

deflection   The amount that something bends out of its regular shape when a force is applied.

distance   The measurable amount that something travels.

fatigue   Harmful wear that surfaces or substances experience due to friction or heat.

first-class lever   A lever that has the fulcrum located between the load and force being applied.

fixed axle   A wheel and axle with the wheel firmly attached to the axle.

fixed pulley   A pulley that is attached to an anchor that provides no mechanical advantage but allows you to change the direction in which the force is applied.

force   The amount of energy that is applied to move something.

free axle   A wheel and axle in which the axle is mounted firmly and the wheel turns freely about it.

friction   The resistance that occurs when one surface slides past another. Friction is increased through surface area, texture, and pressure. The by-products of friction are always heat and wear.

fulcrum   The point on which a lever turns.

fulcrum distance   A term that the author invented to describe the distance between the fulcrum and the load in order to explain how the lever helps to do work.

gear   A wheel that has teeth along its outer edge.

geospools   A term the author coined to describe a board set up like a geoboard but that uses thread spools instead of pegs.

inclined plane   A simple machine that is any sloped surface.

inferring   A scientific process skill that allows someone to draw conclusions from patterns in observations.

interpreting data   A scientific process skill of making mathematical analysis or explaining information gathered through observed events and collected data.

lever   A simple machine that is a bar or rod that pivots on a point known as a fulcrum.

levitate   To rise or float in the air, especially in seeming defiance of gravitation.

load   The amount of mass that you are trying to lift or move.

lubricant   Any substance that is used to reduce friction through reduction of contact between two surfaces passing by each other.

mass   A quantity of matter.

measuring   A scientific process skill that provides statistical data to observations.

mechanical advantage   The amount of help that using a simple machine provides.

movable pulley   A pulley that is attached directly to the load and lifts with it.

moving inclined plane   A simple machine that provides mechanical advantage by its movement under the load rather than the load being moved over its surface.

observing A scientific process skill that is the starting point of data collecting through the use of the senses to learn about objects and events.

pivot To turn on a point.

predicting A scientific process skill that calls for the anticipation of the outcome based on observations and inferences before participating in the event.

pressure The amount of force that holds two objects together.

pulley A wheel and axle combination with a groove in the outside edge of the wheel to hold a line or rope.

results The outcome of experimentation.

rolling friction If one of the surfaces that is coming in contact with an object can roll, then the amount of contact is limited and friction is highly reduced. The rolling surface becomes a wheel and axle.

screw A simple machine that is a combination of a cone and an inclined plane.

second-class lever A bar or rod with the mass located between the force and the fulcrum.

simple machine Any object that helps to do work by being able to trade force for distance. There are three general families: lever, wheel and axle, and inclined plane.

single-beam balance A first-class lever that is used to determine the weight of a mass by placing the unknown on one side of the fulcrum and a known weight on the other side of the fulcrum.

slope The angle at which an inclined plane rests.

spring scale A scale that measures the amount of force being applied by measuring the amount that the spring is being stretched.

sprocket A geared wheel that comes in contact with a chain; or a wheel with holes around the circumference to accommodate spokes.

standard Any measurement system in which all units are equal.

texture The attribute of the surface of a substance.

third-class lever A lever system that has the force applied between the mass and the fulcrum.

threads A spiraling inclined plane that wraps around a cylinder or cone to make the grooves of a bolt or screw.

TMA An abbreviation for Theoretical Mechanical Advantage. This is the mathematical amount of advantage that the simple machine should help you before such factors as friction are involved.

traction The friction between two surfaces that allows for forward movement.

trial Each of the times that you try to do something.

vanes The surfaces that catch wind on a windmill.

wedge A moving inclined plane.

wheel and axle A simple machine made of a bar on which a round frame turns.

windlass A wheel and axle with a spoke or spokes around the perimeter of the wheel used to pull up loads on a rope.

windmill A wheel with vanes around the perimeter that uses the force of the wind as the source of energy.

work Force moving an object across a measurable distance.

INDEX

ABOUT THE AUTHOR

Ralph St. Andre is a native of the Pacific Northwest. Born on a small island called Guemes, his family later moved to Anacortes, Washington, where he attended school until graduation. The area was perfect for the development of his love for hunting, fishing, and roaming in the woods.

St. Andre's desire to become a teacher took him to Western Washington University where he earned his bachelor of arts degree in general science and later completed a master's degree in school administration. To earn his way through university he worked in a plywood mill at night and longshored during the day in the summers. A second job has always been part of his nature. During fifteen of the years he has been in education he has owned and operated a commercial fishing boat.

St. Andre has been in education for 23 years. During that time he has taught in all grades, kindergarten through eighth. He has been a core teacher in grades 5 and 6 as well as a math and science teacher in grades 7 and 8. In 1985, he became a science helping teacher for the Bellingham School District where he facilitated the development of an interactive science kit program for grades K-8. During that process he assisted in the authoring and development of all of the activities. He is currently an elementary principal in Arlington, Washington.

In 1989, St. Andre was named to the ASTC Honor Roll of Science and Technology Teachers. He subsequently received citations from the Washington State House of Representatives and from the Washington State Senate.

St. Andre's family is actively involved in education. His wife Linda has been in elementary education for 23 years and is now an elementary library media specialist for the Bellingham School District. His son Jeff has extended his education at the University of Utah and at Western Washington University. His daughter Suzy is now attending Washington State University.